VE AUG 18

PENGU

THAT GO

TIM FALCONER is the autho. .. *Drive: A Road Trip through Our Complicated Affair with the Automobile* and *Watchdogs and Gadflies: Activism from Marginal to Mainstream*. He teaches magazine writing at Ryerson University and lives in Toronto with his wife.

ALSO BY TIM FALCONER

Watchdogs and Gadflies:
Activism from Marginal to Mainstream

Drive:
A Road Trip through Our Complicated
Affair with the Automobile

TIM FALCONER

THAT GOOD NIGHT

ETHICISTS, EUTHANASIA
AND END-OF-LIFE CARE

PENGUIN
CANADA

PENGUIN CANADA

Published by the Penguin Group

Penguin Group (Canada), 90 Eglinton Avenue East, Suite 700,
    Toronto, Ontario, Canada M4P 2Y3 (a division of Pearson Canada Inc.)

Penguin Group (USA) Inc., 375 Hudson Street, New York, New York 10014, U.S.A.
Penguin Books Ltd, 80 Strand, London WC2R 0RL, England
Penguin Ireland, 25 St Stephen's Green, Dublin 2, Ireland
    (a division of Penguin Books Ltd)
Penguin Group (Australia), 250 Camberwell Road, Camberwell, Victoria 3124, Australia
    (a division of Pearson Australia Group Pty Ltd)
Penguin Books India Pvt Ltd, 11 Community Centre, Panchsheel Park,
    New Delhi – 110 017, India
Penguin Group (NZ), 67 Apollo Drive, Rosedale, North Shore 0632, New Zealand
    (a division of Pearson New Zealand Ltd)
Penguin Books (South Africa) (Pty) Ltd, 24 Sturdee Avenue, Rosebank,
    Johannesburg 2196, South Africa

Penguin Books Ltd, Registered Offices: 80 Strand, London WC2R 0RL, England

First published 2009

1 2 3 4 5 6 7 8 9 10   (WEB)

Copyright © Tim Falconer, 2009

Manufactured in Canada.

Library and Archives Canada Cataloguing in Publication data available
upon request to the publisher.

ISBN: 978-0-670-04455-9

Visit the Penguin Group (Canada) website at **www.penguin.ca**

Special and corporate bulk purchase rates available; please see
www.penguin.ca/corporatesales or call 1-800-810-3104, ext. 477 or 474

FOR MY MOTHER

I am dying with the help of too many physicians.

—Alexander the Great

Contents

A Note to Readers

BECAUSE DEATH is a difficult subject for people to talk about, especially publicly, some of the people I spoke to while researching this book asked for anonymity to preserve their privacy. In some cases, I offered it. When I've given a source a first and last name, that's his or her real name; when I've given a first name only, it's a pseudonym.

1 The Negotiated Death
The rise of the ethicist in an increasingly complicated medical world

MY FATHER was in his late fifties when the doctors diagnosed him with cancer of the esophagus. Within days they performed an eight-hour operation on him and optimistically suggested he had a year to live. After the initial diagnosis, my mother had talked about the two of them travelling while he was still healthy enough to get around; afterwards, when the prognosis had worsened, she started thinking about setting him up in a bed by the front window of our house so he could spend his last days watching the world go by. But he never left the hospital.

The first time I saw my father after the surgery, he was in intensive care. Outside the ICU, before she sent me to his bedside, my mother warned me not to be shocked by what I was about to see; my old man was no longer the vigorous curmudgeon I'd fought with for so many years. He soon made it out of intensive care, but I remember only one visit to his hospital room when he seemed like his old ornery self. Then his health began to deteriorate. Finally, when his condition appeared particularly bad, the doctor took my mother and me aside and started talking in medical gobbledygook; we hadn't a clue what he meant until he translated the jargon: my dad had suffered a stroke.

On a Monday morning in October, just two months after the lengthy operation, the doctor suggested that doing anything other than easing the pain was just postponing the inevitable. We instinctively agreed. Then he suggested we go home to wait—there was nothing for us to do there. So we did. That afternoon, my mother, my four sisters and I watched the Montreal Expos and the Los Angeles Dodgers play the deciding game of the National League Championship Series. In the ninth inning, Rick Monday hit a home run to put the Dodgers ahead 2–1, ending Montreal's dream of making it to the World Series. For Expos fans, that day in 1981 would become known as Blue Monday; for my family, it was even worse. Rick Monday was still trotting around the bases when our phone rang. My mom went upstairs to her bedroom to take the call.

Somehow my father's death didn't teach me much about the subject. I was just twenty-three at the time and it all seemed a weird blur (which may be why that heartbreaking home run looms so large in my memory). Despite many trips to the hospital during his two months there, I didn't really have a sense of watching someone die. And I still wonder why the doctor sent my mother and me home rather than telling us to call my sisters so we could all be around him when he finally died. Maybe the hospital didn't want a bunch of people pacing around like expectant dads (only nervously gloomy instead of excitedly anxious). Up to that point, he certainly didn't look in good shape, but one alarming image I have of that time—and it's one I can't shake, as much as I'd like to—was of him lying helplessly on the bed with the hospital gown askew as he waited for the nurse to re-insert a catheter.

Another image I have of him is from the funeral home. When the folks there asked my family if we wanted an open casket, we took one look at my father and said, "Close it." The body in that box didn't even look like him. A couple of months later, I was at the dry cleaners and the man who owned the place asked where my father was. He seemed shocked to hear the news, because he remembered him always looking so robust.

That my last recollection of my father was so different from the dry cleaner's is no surprise to Robert Buckman, the doctor, author and television personality, who said, "Let me tell you: the last few weeks of someone's life do really imprint upon the memory of the survivors. It's very difficult not to remember them as they were dying in bed."

Even if I didn't care about the people I leave behind when I die—and I do—I don't want to be remembered as a pathetic shadow of my former self. And since I don't even want to be a shadow of my former self, I fear the process of dying a lot more than death itself. Like most people, I suppose. But I have taken the time to imagine my grand exit: I'll be playing hockey, many, many years from now, and after scoring a highlight-reel goal—top corner, glove side—I'll go to the bench and quietly keel over. I have no idea what my father's ideal death would have been. Given that he was a gunner in the Second World War, I'm sure he'd thought about dying at some point in his life, but I don't know if he ever thought about how he would have liked to die. Perhaps my dad would have wanted to drop dead on the links after a hole-in-one. (We buried him in a green jacket with the insignia of his golf club on the breast pocket.)

My father didn't get his ace or his perfect demise. But while I can't say he went gently, his death was a relatively simple and straightforward one as these things go. (And because he died when he was in his fifties and not in his nineties, the Presbyterian church where he had been an elder had to set up an overflow room to accommodate all his friends who showed up at the funeral despite the torrential October rain that day.) Two months is not a long time to struggle with cancer and my father never really knew what hit him. But even without the complications, it was a negotiated death. And like most Canadians these days, he didn't die at home. In fact, according to a study led by Daren Heyland of Queen's University, 73 percent of Canadians die in hospital or another medical setting. Unless we die suddenly from something like a heart attack, by our own hand or in a fatal car crash, most of us will suffer an institutional death (though it's also true that hospitals are no longer so keen to send families home, so we may not have to face our time of dying alone). "Death—for the first time in history—is now largely a negotiated event," according to Kerry Bowman, the clinical bioethicist at Mount Sinai Hospital in Toronto. "If a person is on life-support machines, what are we going to do if they get pneumonia? Are we going to decrease the ventilator settings? What if the kidneys fail? It's a form of negotiation."

More than that, these negotiations increasingly turn on thorny and uncomfortable ethical dilemmas, ones many of us don't feel completely qualified to deal with. "So we're in new terrain," added Bowman, "and it's hard on everybody."

"WHAT WAS THE MOST AMAZING THING that took place in your lifetime?" I asked my mom a year or two after my father died.

She answered right away, almost as if she'd been expecting the question. "A man landing on the moon," she said. Then, after a brief pause, she added, "And seeing it on television."

It was a sensible answer for someone who was born just a few years after Charles Lindbergh made history with his solo transatlantic flight in the *Spirit of St. Louis* and a few years before RCA showed off the television at the 1939 World's Fair. But I was a TV junkie, born a year after the Soviet Union sparked the space race by launching Sputnik, so watching the moon shot didn't have the same air of unbelievability for me. Sure, I thought it was pretty neat—and I did write as many school projects on the space program as I could—but I was hardly surprised or really amazed.

I often mull over my own question, but I can never decide how to answer it, because technological advances have always seemed so expected during my lifetime. I considered human cloning—which, when it finally happens, will be a case of science fiction coming true, just as to previous generations a man on the moon was—but now it seems like it will be anti-climactic.

Still, when someone really does pull it off, the feat will be impressive, though not necessarily in a good way. There were, of course, a few naysayers back in 1969 who were convinced the Apollo 11 mission was a hoax, but the vast majority of people celebrated Neil Armstrong's giant leap for mankind as much as they did his small step. Human cloning, on the other hand, presents so many ethical problems that the detractors are sure to swamp the defenders. Most people have watched the cloning of animals—including a sheep and a monkey—with a weird mix of detachment and resignation. We're not sure all this "progress" is a good thing, but we also doubt there's anything we can do about it, especially since we don't really understand it. A few people—mostly academics and specialists who call themselves ethicists—do debate issues such as cloning, but too often they do so at such a rarefied level that the rest of us are left a little dizzy.

Like most people, I consider myself ethical. And also like most people, I took it for granted that I was ethical and never gave it much thought—until, that is, Ross Rebagliati won a gold medal in snowboarding at the 1998 Winter Olympics in Nagano. Along with most Canadians, I was thrilled. He was, after all, a bright, articulate and stylish guy engaged in a hip new sport—and best of all, he was a winner wearing our colours. But a day later, his drug test came back positive for marijuana.

As sporting scandals go, it had nothing on the commotion over sprinter Ben Johnson testing positive for steroids after winning the 100-metre dash, the most prestigious event in Olympic competition. But what fascinated me was that when the news about Rebagliati hit, one of the first places many newspaper reporters and television producers called was the Canadian Centre for Ethics in Sports (CCES). After all, the fate of a snowboarder who might have smoked a little weed is hardly a matter of great importance, even if the great French author Albert Camus did write, "I learned all I know about ethics from sports."

The journalists probably didn't think twice about calling the Ottawa-based CCES, so common had the phrase "Ethicists say..."—usually followed by a quote from a university professor—already become in the media. That made people such as Dr. Andrew Pipe—who helped start the Canadian Centre for Drug-Free Sport (which soon became the CCES) and served as the organization's chair for twelve years before stepping down in 2004—obvious sources for harried newshounds. It didn't matter that the reporters probably didn't have the time or the inclination to wonder why they needed to call an ethicist about what was, really, just another controversy in the controversy-riddled annals of sports.

And one thing's for sure: we don't need to be ethicists to have lots of loud fun debating such scandals over a beer in a bar. But plenty of what ethicists worry about is complicated. Bioethics is the most highly developed specialty within the field, and issues such as cloning, genetic engineering and euthanasia—to name just a few—are fraught with complexities and competing interests. So it's no surprise that bioethics leads other ethical disciplines in terms of the amount of literature, number of university courses devoted to it and job opportunities. Or that the Canadian Bioethics Society, a group formed in 1988 with the amalgamation of the Canadian Society of Bioethics and the Canadian Society for Medical Ethics, has over six hundred members, including doctors, nurses, lawyers, philosophers, theologians and health care administrators. But interest in ethics is also surging elsewhere, including in business, government and the military. Attention to such "practical ethics" (sometimes known by the more misleading term "applied ethics") has come so far that there are now two national organizations—the Ethics Practitioners Association of Canada and the Canadian Society for the Study of Practical Ethics—devoted to this growth industry.

Business, which is just a duller, more mature version of sports, has glommed onto ethics with mercenary glee. Inevitably, a lot of people are cynical about business ethics and figure most companies would rather be seen as ethical than actually act ethically. And skepticism about the worth of business ethics only increased when Paul Coffin, the advertising executive convicted of stealing $1.5 million in the federal sponsorship scandal, lectured McGill University students on the subject as part of a sentence that included no jail time.

Of course, we've come to expect some of the most blatant ethical breaches from government. While lots of people know there's a federal ethics commissioner, fewer know that almost every federal department has an ethics officer and that many have programs to educate public servants in basic ethical principles about honesty, conflict of interest and so on. Nevertheless, over the last couple of decades, the big electoral changes have resulted from questionable ethics. First, Brian Mulroney swept away years of Liberal corruption and cronyism in 1984 by wagging his finger at John Turner, Pierre Trudeau's hapless successor, and saying, "You did have an option, sir." Nine years later, Jean Chrétien's Liberals crushed the Progressive Conservatives, who had faced scandal after scandal during Mulroney's turn. And in 2006, the Liberals collapsed under the weight of AdScam and other boondoggles, making Conservative Stephen Harper prime minister.

Meanwhile, personal ethics—which can run the gamut from fairly banal questions about when, if ever, it is okay to lie to a loved one, all the way up to life-and-death decisions—is another growth industry. The ethics column is now a standard feature in newspapers: readers write in with ethical dilemmas and some self-appointed know-it-all tells them what they should do. Human relations have always been complicated and, in many ways, these columns aren't much different than Ann Landers and Dear Abby, except the responses usually aren't so uptight and dogmatic. Still, their popularity suggests that a lot of people are hungry for some guidance in their lives—and apparently many of them would rather listen to anyone other than the clergy.

FOR CENTURIES, there was just one right way to do things. The Church dictated right and wrong, good and evil, so ethics were easy. Most Canadians still believe in some form of god, but even for many of them, organized religion long ago slipped into irrelevance or—in the wake of appallingly frequent child abuse scandals—worse. So that's the last place many of us want to go for help. In addition, our society is now more pluralistic. Instead of being a country full of Christians, modern Canada is home to practising and lapsed Catholics and Protestants, Muslims, Buddhists and people of many other faiths and beliefs, including a growing flock of atheists. In fact, according to *Fire and Ice: The United States, Canada and the Myth of Converging Values*, by Michael Adams, nearly four in ten Canadians do not adhere to a religious faith.

So we're losing our religion, but that doesn't really explain why we're turning to these new ethical arbiters. After all, Americans are, if anything, further along into the ethics boom than we are, even though religion remains a great deal more central to their lives than it is to ours. In *Fire and Ice*, Adams tells us that only 22 percent of Canadians claim to attend church services on a weekly basis—down from 60 percent in the 1950s—and only 30 percent say religion is important to them. By contrast, 42 percent of Americans go to church every Sunday and 59 percent say religion is important in their lives.

Despite the Canadian stats, I was curious what Rev. Canon Eric Beresford thought about our need for guidance from ethicists. He came to Canada from his native England for a summer visit when he was in his twenties and ended up staying. After holding positions in Anglican Church parishes, he taught ethics at McGill's faculty of religious studies. The church hired him back in 1996 to become its ethics coordinator—though one of the first things he did was change his title to ethics consultant: "How am I supposed to coordinate anybody's ethics when I can hardly coordinate my own? What I can do is be a consultant."

We met in a nondescript room in the Anglican Church House in central Toronto. The bare white walls left me with the impression that we were in the middle of a blank slate. That seemed about right. Beresford, who later left Toronto for Halifax to become the president of the Atlantic School of Theology, first answered the question I *didn't* ask. "What we don't need ethicists for is to tell us what the right thing to do is," he said. "Moral decision making is, in fact, something we all already do before we ever meet an ethicist. We don't need an ethicist to tell us we need to be moral in the way we do things."

He went on to explain what ethicists can do: help us understand the nature and history of the ethical arguments we all use and to understand some of the unforeseen implications or consequences of those arguments. Ethicists can also help the conversation along. "When people are involved in a conflict, the last thing they're very good at is really hearing the people they're arguing with. It's a dialogue of the deaf. So one of the tasks of ethicists is to assist in the hearing."

Of course, there's nothing new about people not listening to each other, and I've seen no evidence that people want to be better listeners. In fact, if the inane crossfire between political partisans—especially, but certainly not exclusively, south of the border—is any indication, we'd rather just scream at each other.

But clearly something is going on. "The growth in interest in ethics almost always parallels a time of cultural crisis," said Beresford. To make his point he cited *Nicomachean Ethics*, a book Aristotle wrote to justify the virtues of Athens, even as those virtues were under threat. As the city-state became the centre of an empire, it sucked in wealth and new cultural influences that resulted in dramatic changes to Athenian society. "When that happens, the assumptions about the old way of doing things don't hold any longer. There was a crisis and Aristotle was responding to the crisis."

Beresford believes we are once again in a period of cultural upheaval. "When I was going to university, people thought science was the be-all and end-all. It could do anything, solve everything, take us anywhere. People are increasingly skeptical of that. They have seen that many of the innovations of science have come with an unadvertised cost."

THE MODERN ETHICS MOVEMENT started in the 1950s and '60s with the debate over medical ethics. In 1954, Joseph Fletcher published *Morals and Medicine*. Fletcher was an Episcopalian priest, though he later renounced his belief in God, became an atheist and eventually served as president of the Euthanasia Society of America (the forerunner of the Society for the Right to Die). Some people see him as the father of bioethics, but his book was more influential in some circles (theologians and philosophers) than in others (the medical community). But doctors would soon have no choice but to join the discussion. During the First and Second World Wars, the need to get soldiers back fighting led to many medical advances. Then in the 1950s, we saw the introduction of the modern ventilator, the beginnings of modern immunology, which made organ transplants possible, and other innovations. In the early 1960s, the development of the dialysis machine created a dilemma over access to the new technology. For the first time in history, it wasn't just doctors making decisions—it was a group of hospital administrators, theologians and medical staff trying to develop criteria to decide who would get this life-saving treatment.

Meanwhile, in the aftermath of revelations about the Nazis' human experimentation, outrage grew over research involving human subjects in the United States. Two clinical trials were particularly shocking. From 1963 to 1966, scientists injected developmentally disabled students at Willowbrook State School with the virus that causes hepatitis and then followed the course of the disease. And in the Tuskegee Syphilis Study, which ran from 1932 to 1972 and used black sharecroppers as its subjects, researchers—without seeking informed consent from patients, or even telling them they had syphilis—withheld penicillin from them. After the media broke the story, the scientists shut down the study, but public outrage led to the creation of the National Commission for the Protection of Human Subjects of Biomedical and Behavioral Research. The commission's findings, called the Belmont Report, identified three ethical principles that should govern research on human subjects: respect for persons, beneficence and justice.

With these developments, people who weren't doctors started to have influence over how doctors did their jobs. But this mix of experts needed a new vocabulary. And this led to the rise of the bioethicist. In the 1980s and '90s, the profession—which expanded its repertoire to include everything from genomics to nanotechnology—grew dramatically. And the fascination with ethics spread beyond medicine. "The conversation that started in the fifties and sixties was about medical ethics," said Beresford, "and now there are ethicists all over the place, and it's not quite clear what they all do or why they do it."

Beresford and I spoke for two hours, and while he started off with a great deal of energy, he began to flag before ninety minutes was up and by the end seemed exhausted. But he finished by talking about his skepticism toward the ethics explosion. He'd already told me he feared that ethicists were being accepted as experts in a way they really weren't. "Their moral judgments are all too often being used to close debate rather than to explore why there's significant moral disagreement and debate in a particular area." The motivation for using ethicists is anxiety, he said. "And the danger is ethicists become the ones who resolve anxiety by excluding some of the values that stand in conflict to each other."

In addition, he worried that ethicists were overwhelmingly middle-class and—until relatively recently, overwhelmingly white—men (the majority still are). "Now, there's nothing wrong with being white and male and middle-class," he said, "but it is rather a narrow view of the world." And as a middle-class white guy, he wasn't letting himself off the hook either. So his final thought to me was: "I want to acknowledge that I get paid to do this stuff. I am one of the beneficiaries of the increased interest in ethics, but I recognize that I am part of a machine that might not be doing things that are entirely appropriate."

NOT THAT I HAD ANY DOUBTS, but a business ethicist convinced me ethics aren't simple. The task wasn't that difficult for David Nitkin; he just had to give me an oral exam. Nitkin, the head of a Toronto-based consultancy called EthicScan Canada Limited and the founding president of the Ethics Practitioners Association of Canada, has been a business ethicist since 1988, longer than anyone else in the country. And yet, when I arrived at the address he gave me, I had to double-check it to make sure I had the right spot. His modest home in the city's inner suburbs had an overgrown tree out front with low-hanging branches and certainly didn't look like a building that contained an office with employees. In fact, it looked like a house kids might run past on Halloween. It was the right place, though, and as I waited in the kitchen for him to come up from his basement office, his wife was busy baking a cake.

He didn't put me on the spot right away, but after telling me about his company, about himself and about his approach to ethics, he outlined the case of a client that had won a lucrative consulting contract to work on China's massive Three Gorges Dam project. Soon, though, the firm started fearing a headline in *The Globe and Mail* along the lines of: "Canadian company complicit in slave labour." This is the classic sniff test, also known as an integrity test: how comfortable would an organization feel if a story about its actions appeared on the front page of the newspapers? The company had discovered that the Communist Party regularly forced local men and women to move rock by hand and paid them nothing. Knowing his firm's ethical principles included doing nothing illegal and respecting human life, the chief engineer raised the issue with the Chinese government, but the official he contacted denied it, while also insisting the engineer didn't understand Chinese culture and tradition. The official also warned him that if he mentioned it again, the contract would go to a competitor who wouldn't ask uncomfortable questions. The company came to Nitkin and said, "David, don't tell us we have to leave this contract, but what do we do?"

As I sat at the kitchen table, I innocently asked, "So your advice was?"

"Well, you tell me what you'd do."

I paused. Then, with more self-righteousness than confidence, I said: "My advice would be to get out, but that's obviously not an option."

"Well, it's an option, but not one they wanted to hear," he explained. "Does that help the labourers? All you're going to do is get someone with fewer qualms who's going to go in and do the contract. So you failed ethics test number one. Ethics test number two: same particulars. What do you recommend to the company?"

My pause was longer this time. I looked at his feet, in white socks, no shoes. I looked at the white patch in his beard, at his wire-rim glasses and his salt-and-pepper hair. Nowhere did I see the answer. "Well, I guess they're going to have to apply some pressure to the government."

"Diinnggg. Doesn't work. The government is going to tell them they've lost the contract. I mean, I'm talking about professional, knowledgeable experience, not pie in the sky. Same set of issues, same question. Chance number three."

I let out a deep and pained sigh, followed by a really long pause. I wished I could be anywhere but there and I felt like insisting that I was there to ask questions, not answer them. Somehow, though, I didn't think he'd care about that and I finally sputtered, "I don't know, find a way to make that kind of labour unnecessary ..."

"Change the Chinese culture?"

"No, bring in equipment or whatever that would make moving rocks by hand unnecessary."

"Closer," he allowed. I started to feel a bit relieved, but he wasn't about to let me off just yet. "So where do you go from here?"

"I don't know."

"Well, I'm not going to pay you $12,000 a year to tell me you don't know."

As it turns out, Nitkin advised the company to give earth-moving equipment to the different communities as a cultural investment. That way, on the days when people had to work on the project, they'd be able to use machines rather than their hands. On other days, the workers could use the equipment for their own projects.

Along with taking me down a peg or two, Nitkin had made his point: ethics consulting doesn't have to be flakey or light-weight (despite the impression I had after meeting some putative business ethicists). And it's not simply common sense. Even people who see themselves as ethical, who think about ethics— even people who write about ethics—find it hard to distinguish what's ethical and what's not. Just as there are people who see everything as political, there are those who view everything as a question of ethics. But Nitkin isn't one of them.

I cited an example from "The Ethicist," the popular and long-running *New York Times Magazine* column written by Randy Cohen, who is not a trained ethicist. The question he examined one week was whether it was ethical to drive up an empty highway exit lane and then cut back into a lane of stop-and-go traffic further up the road. As much as I enjoy Cohen's answers, this question struck me as better suited to a column on manners and etiquette than one on ethics. While other ethicists later suggested that it could be an ethical question if there was a safety issue involved, Nitkin agreed with me. "That's not about ethics. That's about mores, that's about the law, that's about values. It isn't about ethics," he said, pointing out that part of his job is to separate the ethical problems from ones that are about personal conviction or law or etiquette or personal choice or whatever. "Not all of today's problems are about ethics."

He explained the difference between four basic, but often confused, concepts: law, values, morality and ethics. The law is what's legally sanctioned. Some laws may be antiquated or generally not respected by the public (most people drive over the speed limit on major highways, for example). "The law may be transgressed by criminals or by people like Gandhi who put themselves up as conscientious objectors," Nitkin explained. "But it is determined by lawyers and politicians and it does represent one standard of right and wrong." Values are quite different. We learn them at our mother's knee, and they are not necessarily about right and wrong. Instead, they may be basic concepts such as respect for the environment, respect for truth, or an interest in material acquisitions. Someone might value a Mercedes or a cottage. These are things that are important and significant to a person and they tend not to change. Morality, on the other hand—which is about perceptions of right and wrong—does change. We've seen moral attitudes toward pre-marital sex and homosexuality, for example, change in a single generation. As well, morality often varies from place to place. The attitude toward same-sex marriage differs greatly between downtown Toronto and rural Bible-Belt communities.

By contrast, Nitkin sees ethics as principles that cross cultures as well as time. What's ethical and what's not doesn't depend on religion, upbringing or culture. Ethics, in a business setting, for example, are about a standard definition of what a company wants its employees to do. "Organizational ethics are fixed by the organization in consensual terms with employees. They're understood by all and they are communicated in the same way—in an ethical organization."

MANY BIOETHICISTS would love to be able to see ethics as simply a choice between right and wrong. But for them it's often a choice between two rights—or two wrongs. "Ethics," according to Kerry Bowman, a white, middle-class male bioethicist, "is often about picking the best of some pretty bad options."

He showed me what he meant when I sat in on his philosophy course at York University. Called Health Care Ethics, it attracted people who worked in the health care field but also some, including a couple of film students, who didn't. Since Bowman doesn't drive a car—he gets around Toronto on an old bike or, especially in the winter, uses public transit—I picked him up at a subway station on a cold January evening after a snowstorm. Arriving at the university by car instead of bus, Bowman was disoriented and we spent a lot of time driving around the large, wind-swept suburban campus as he tried to figure out where his building was. In the end, we parked much farther away than we needed to and laughed about his orienteering skills as we hiked in through the fresh snow.

The first half of the class was devoted to two student presentations—one on the ethics of treating mental illness, one on stem cell research. Then, after announcing the topic for the second half of the evening—ethical questions in the discovery of mistaken paternity—he gave the students a break. I took the interruption as an opportunity to ask some of the students what they thought of Bowman as a teacher. They were clearly all fans and appreciated that he cared about both them and the material. One student said, "He's the best teacher I have this year." To which another added, "Best ever."

When everyone returned to the cheerless classroom with its cinderblock walls and small windows, Bowman leaned with one hand on a computer cart and addressed the nineteen students sitting in plastic chairs. His hospital ID cards still dangled around his neck. He asked the class to split into two groups and he presented, as the slide projected on the screen explained, "The Case of George." The patriarch of a quiet, conservative and religious family, George, a fifty-eight-year-old widower, wanted to donate a kidney to his twenty-one-year-old son, who had serious renal disease. The doctors arranged a genetic test to ensure compatibility, but the test revealed something unexpected: there was no genetic relationship between father and son. "What do you do and why, using an ethical rationale?" Bowman asked the class. "Would you tell this man? Would you tell this son? Would you tell neither? And why would you do it?"

Bowman explained that this was not as rare as we might think; in fact, one study indicated that as much as 10 percent of human paternity is mistaken or misrepresented. But he wouldn't say anything more because he didn't want to sway the class (he's found the more he talks, the more he sways).

I sat in with one group and listened as a woman said that for reasons of transparency and potential future medical implications, she would tell the father and son they weren't related. As Bowman, who moved between the two groups, joined us, a man who worked in a hospital suggested the doctors needed only to say that the father's kidneys were not compatible; it wasn't their job to explain why they weren't compatible. "You know what?" said Bowman. "Our lawyer would agree with you one hundred percent, and that's almost exactly what he said. 'Why on earth would you want to get into this tangle? You legally don't have to,' he told us. But ethics is what we ought to do, rather than what we have to do."

Then Bowman further complicated the discussion by explaining that the father scored three out of six on the compatibility test, meaning the two men weren't related but that a transplant was possible. That meant that on top of the psychological damage to both father and son and the possible destruction of the family, there was the possibility that the father would refuse to donate his kidney to the young man, even though a transplant was likely to be a success. Bowman then asked us, "Do you think these two people want to know? Or do you think they would ask why on earth you had dropped a hydrogen bomb on their lives?"

Our discussion continued until Bowman asked the circle of students what they'd decided. Only the man who worked in a hospital wouldn't tell the father and son they weren't related. His take was that the absence of paternity was an incidental finding, so there was no need to tell. Then Bowman called me out: "Tim, do you want to weigh in on this? Let's get a pragmatic journalist's approach here."

"Well, pragmatically, I wouldn't tell," I said, "but ethically, I guess I'd have to. But I wouldn't want to be the one to have to do it."

The conversation continued for several more minutes until I came up with a stray intelligent thought. "Kerry, is it really informed consent if the father doesn't know the truth—if either of them doesn't know?"

"That's a really good question. Is it truly informed consent? The medical risk of the surgery is informed, but does informed consent extend to the emotional, psycho-social context? Most people would say it probably does."

When Bowman brought the class back together, it turned out that the other group was the mirror opposite of ours. With one exception, they all agreed they wouldn't inform the men they weren't related. But they'd decided that on the understanding that the kidneys weren't compatible, so all they had to tell the patients was that a donation wasn't possible. To that, Bowman pointed out that it might not take the men much time on the internet to figure out why.

He went on to explain that this sort of ethical dilemma was uncommon in the past but now comes up more because of the prevalence of genetic testing, especially since doctors began routinely testing unborn children for genetic abnormalities— and (if the study he'd mentioned earlier is accurate) being surprised in one out of ten cases. In response, some hospitals have started to rewrite consent forms to explain that the genetic test may reveal that the paternity is not what the parents thought it was. "People burst out laughing. They think they're on *Candid Camera* or something," explained Bowman. "Sometimes they are the very people who aren't related to who they think they are. We can't get people to take it seriously, yet we also have this haunting 10 percent data."

As the class discussion continued, the other group carried on making its case until Bowman said, "You guys are building some nice arguments for not telling, but I ask you, how could this not be paternalism? Paternalism is what our entire health care system is trying to move away from because we found it morally difficult, to say the least. Is it not paternalistic to say I'm going to make this decision on your behalf because I think you'll be better off in the long run even though you don't know it?" He added that it's rare for doctors to come across medical information that they don't tell their patients and that full disclosure is at the heart of autonomy, another central value in our health care system.

In the end, Bowman was happy that the class divided so strongly on the dilemma (though I wondered how much of that was a result of some manipulation on his part). He noted that hospitals appeared to be moving toward adopting a case-by-case approach that considers social, cultural and individual factors. That would mean having to make a lot of highly subjective and judgmental decisions, but a blanket disclosure policy brought with it the danger that women who weren't sure of the paternity of their babies might not get the necessary genetic testing.

Finally, he left the class with something to ponder: "God forbid, but I just have to do this as a thought experiment: if there was misunderstood paternity in our lives, meaning our fathers, would you want to know? You don't have to answer that—this is not that kind of class—but it brings it home."

FOR BRINGING THINGS HOME, nothing beats seeing a family member on his or her deathbed and having to make a difficult ethical choice. Helping patients and families negotiate death would be hard enough in a monoculture; it's even more difficult with the increasing cultural diversity of Canadian society. Mount Sinai, for example, is in downtown Toronto and the cultural backgrounds of its patients reflect the diversity of the city. "The framework for negotiating death is barely present even for white-bread Anglo-Saxons," Kerry Bowman said to me. "So you take people from places where death is seen as something absolutely divine or in the hands of something else, and you ask these families to enter a negotiation." Here he let out a huge breath. "This can be profoundly difficult for people. They don't want anything to do with it. It feels wrong. It fits better in Western culture, where we medicalize things. Control is a big issue in Western culture. It fits better for us, but for a lot of other people, it's a living nightmare and they don't want to touch it. And you can't blame them."

In the case of my father—a white-bread Anglo-Saxon, to be sure—there was no disagreement, or really even any debate, between his family and his medical team. Nevertheless, the timing of his death was "negotiated" as soon as we agreed the doctor should do nothing but try to control the pain.

Aside from how shocked I would have been to see my mother acting out of character—she is, above all, a practical woman—I don't know what would have happened if she had argued with the doctor's recommendation, if she had pleaded with him or ranted that he was just making that decision to save money. This was 1981, after all, when everyone, including impractical people, was reluctant to argue with doctors, and when even large hospitals like the one my father died in didn't have ethicists on staff to help us grapple with all the ethical issues and, if necessary, play mediator between a family and the medical team. We wouldn't have had a clue what an ethicist did anyway.

Even today, most families who watch a loved one die do so without ever talking to an expert in these matters. But clinical ethicists are now common, in major hospitals at least, though the job still isn't widely understood by the general public. If I had any doubts about this, they vanished when I followed Bowman to Sudbury, Ontario, to watch him speak about his other passion: ape conservation in Africa. While giving an afternoon talk, Bowman mentioned his day job. Afterward, some people gathered around him to ask questions. A couple of them were puzzled: one woman wanted to check that he really did say he was an anaesthetist, and when he explained that he's actually an ethicist, another woman said, "Oh, I thought you said you were an aesthetician."

Later, he had a good laugh about it, but it was also a reminder that the nature of his profession remains murky to most people. After all, most deaths are negotiated without the help of an ethicist. And although he has worked on hundreds of end-of-life cases, not every dilemma a clinical ethicist faces is a life-or-death situation. He also deals with issues such as organ transplants, hospital policy and the duty to care. But one way or another, death figures prominently in the job. And given that most people are more than a little blurry on the differences between withdrawing treatment ("pulling the plug"), giving mom a little more morphine than she really needs not just to ease the pain but to speed the inevitable along, assisted suicide and euthanasia, maybe ethicists can come in handy.

With or without ethicists, we have decisions to make, both as individuals and as a society. Most of us remember Dylan Thomas's "Do not go gentle into that good night" from high school. In 1951, the Welsh poet called on his father, a once robust army man who had become frail and blind in his eighties, to "rage, rage against the dying of the light." Today, some children still want that for their elderly parents, but many others hope only for an ending that is as peaceful and painless as possible—for their parents and, when the time comes, themselves.

Each year, more than 225,000 people die in Canada. Most do not go gently. Advances in medical technology and know-how, combined with the aging of our population, have seen to that. And most families make whatever decisions they must without the help of a clinical ethicist. But while we can keep people alive longer, that doesn't mean we're comfortable with the dilemmas that inevitably arise. "As difficult as it is having death as a negotiated event—and I don't mean to be harsh about this—we're going to have to get used to it," Bowman warned. "We've got to throw our hearts and heads into this, because it's going to get more complicated, not less."

And so, with Bowman as my main guide, I set out to learn about the way we die, a journey that meant hearing many moving stories and inevitably led me to confront assisted suicide and euthanasia. Although most of us will knock on heaven's door without any ethicists ever hearing our names (and, frankly, we should all hope for that) we may find ethical expertise helpful as our society finally faces the prospect of legalizing the right to die the way we want. But as responsible citizens, we—not ethicists or doctors, activists or politicians—must decide.

2 Hastening the Inevitable
A son's struggle to do what's best for his parents

TERRY'S PARENTS DIED within a few months of each other and in both cases he watched—and to a certain extent participated in— those deaths. Three years later, when I spoke to him, the subject was still a sensitive one for him, but it was not nearly as raw as it had been, and I found him uncommonly reflective about his experience. Unlike some people, whose parents die in big-city hospitals, Terry and his brother and sister did not have the benefit of a clinical ethicist to help them grapple with their decision. But grapple they did, especially with the difficult questions that increasingly come with a negotiated death, including deciding when life is no longer worth prolonging, when to withdraw care and how far to go in hastening the inevitable.

Here, in his own words, is what he told me:

Just before Christmas, they were two normal people dealing with being older. They were both born in 1923 and my mother straddled the life of char lady and lady of the estate. She washed her own clothes, did all her own gardening and never could get the earth out of her hands if she ever had to completely clean up. But she'd still fit in a book and tea at four. I remember her sitting in the sunshine with a cup of tea outside in the garden of the house that she loved, looking like a million bucks. She had been a tennis champion as a kid and she was physically active in that way that you are when you walk a lot and garden a lot, but she wasn't physically active in a twenty-first-century way of jogging and running and workouts. I took her to Europe when she was in her late sixties and I made it conditional on her having a full checkup. That was just me being bossy, but that was the first time she'd visited a doctor for a full medical since my brother was born. And she had a completely clean checkup.

My father was one of those people with great genes. He'd had such extraordinary health all his life. A few abscessed teeth—that's about all he ever had to complain about. He went in for a checkup at sixty because I'd encouraged him to go. I'd sort of read him the riot act. And the doctor in a glib way said, "You're good for another ten years."

So he didn't go back.

He would come to Toronto to visit me for a weekend and he'd get to know more people in the neighbourhood than I do. After one of those visits, I was at the butcher shop and the butcher said, "Has your dad been in for a prostate checkup because my father-in-law is busy dying of it and it's insidious but it can be dealt with if it's caught soon enough." So, knowing my father, I sent him a fax saying, "Please look up the latest *Time* magazine. Page 39." It was a big article about all the well-known people in the world who were dying of prostate cancer and all about the disease.

He took himself off for a checkup and it was stage four, which means it had already gotten into his body. They removed his testicles and he got about eight years of relief from the drug therapy. At Christmastime, he went into hospital basically for plumbing maintenance. Then he was back home, but he wasn't able to get up and down stairs easily. He was showing his age finally. In his mid-seventies, he'd looked like he was in his mid-sixties. But all of a sudden he was losing weight and you could tell that he was shifting into a new phase of the illness where he was not bouncing back.

My mother was just resolute about going forward and wanting to keep his spirits up. She was in a reasonable state of denial about it being in the late stages. Between Christmas and April, he went to the hospital a few times for checkups and stuff. And in April my mother caught pneumonia, they think just from going to the hospital with my dad.

My wife, Carol, and I were down for the weekend and Mum looked tired and coughed like you would if you had a cold or the flu or something. She spent Monday in bed, which she never would do. My mother was never sick, was never interested in medical care. She was so constitutionally strong and resistant to medical attention. The pneumonia had turned into meningitis and within a week she was in a coma-like state.

Monday she was in bed. Wednesday night she went to the hospital. Thursday I was there with my brother and with my sister. Saturday, she was done. We didn't talk to her after that. She was in full-blown, serious, we-might-lose-her illness. She was unconscious, her heart was going like crazy, she was sweating. She was in intensive care, they were giving her drips and medicines and all that stuff. I was up all night putting wet cloths on her.

A machine was making her heart beat, and they said she might last a month and she wouldn't get better. But she defied all their odds about how she was going to die—that she might get over the pneumonia but the infections in the hospital would kill her. None of that happened. She completely got over the pneumonia and her heart was back beating for itself and she survived the meningitis, but she had brain damage.

She was on some morphine and a feeding tube because she couldn't swallow. As her illness protracted, she started to get all this tightness of her arms and legs. She looked like a stroke person in the sense that her toes and her hands and her arms were all in great tension. It was as if she was paralyzed. They did physiotherapy but she was basically in a very rigid state. If someone tried to move her arms, she'd wince. Her mouth would open and close, but she couldn't talk, and if someone tried to brush her teeth, she'd try to close her mouth. There was no engagement. We got the best talent in the area to come and see her and they all described her as in a vegetative state. Beyond saying, "This is not your mum anymore," they were questioning whether she was really there at all.

We always treated her as if she was there. I would walk in and say, "Hi, Mum, how are you?" and fiddle with the flowers. I'd put her glasses on, but her eyes would not hold me, they would look all over the room and not engage me in any way.

Later, I put our baby on her lap, put her rigid fingers on the baby's hands. Physically, I got to know my mother in a way I never had and I don't mean just that I cut her fingernails. I would spend hours rubbing her hair and her face and hugging her and holding her hand. I would hold her hand for hours. I loved my mum but I'd never had that kind of physical relation-ship with her. And it was very intense.

I'd be very resolute about going and very organized. I'd fly down there and get my car because it's an hour's drive from the airport. And then I'd just not want to go. It was like facing something deeply unpleasant and scary and I just didn't want to do it. It was nervousness, like you're about to break up with someone or someone is about to break up with you. It's coming and it's awful. But then I'd go in and see her, say hi and then I didn't want to leave her. There was that physical intimacy that this is a boy and his mum. And the seductive thing about walking in and seeing her asleep. She looked twenty years younger asleep. So I'd find myself thinking, "She's okay, she's going to wake up in a minute. It's not true, it's not real."

Of course, sometimes I'd walk in and she'd be looking around the room. Her head wouldn't move, her eyes would open and her mouth would be open but there wouldn't be any of the expressions I'd recognize. I remember coming home from the hospital and coming back to the house and crying and crying. What triggered it was I saw her handwriting and realized she'd never write again. These were letters I got at boarding school with a beautiful, beautiful blue pen on blue paper. That was a tangible sense of loss.

In April, I had my mother in a bed in intensive care and my father in a bed at the other end of the hospital because he'd been admitted with pneumonia as well. His wasn't as advanced and he got through it. But from being completely robust a year earlier, he was at a very declining stage where he'd lost a pile of weight and wasn't as strong. The cancer by that point was right through his bones. It was very evident to my brother, my sister and me—and my father—that he was in the later stages of cancer. He'd set himself a goal of getting to eighty and he was seventy-eight, but he shortened his horizons to just maybe making it to Christmas.

In June, he saw an article in *The Globe and Mail* about this guy in Halifax [John Connolly of Dalhousie University's Faculty of Medicine] doing research using some techniques that go back seventy years, where basically they wire up the brain so they can check brainwaves. So this guy figured out that if you asked questions, where half of them are nonsense—some of them would be like, "The pizza was too hot to sing"—if you've got a functioning brain in there it doesn't like that, so it gets more active.

My dad happened to read this article and we got the hospital to send my mum down to Halifax in an ambulance. I mean, the poor man has got his heart broken. He knows he's not long for this world, but he did all these things, like build a wheelchair ramp at the house so my mum could move home. It was hope.

I did crazy things too. When we had her in Halifax, I flew down and got her in a wheelchair, checked her out of the hospital, took her to the Public Gardens, which she would have known as a kid and we'd visited as a family. I pushed her around and ordered her an ice cream cone. "Want some ice cream, Mum? What do you like? Vanilla? I'll get some of that." I held it up and she licked at the ice cream cone. It was like a boy and his invalid mum but I didn't really know what was there. Then I felt guilty because I had to make a phone call and she was just sitting there, staring into space. I pushed her around pointing out the trees and flowers, talking about the family or whatever. A really rational person would say that she was fried, that she was not there. But then there's that great story about the French guy who wrote a whole book with his eyelash.

At one point, we'd taken her off morphine for a while because people said maybe that was dulling her consciousness. We weren't guinea-pigging her but, retrospectively, I worry that we might have contributed to more pain. It's terrible to think about that. Also, when we had her in Halifax—I'm unhappy about this now—they put her under some quite aggressive physiotherapy trying to get her to sit up. And I got caught up in all this care, but now, with perspective, I would say why bother? She was not going to ever walk again, she was never going to be herself again. But at the time I was saying, "Oh my God, this is rehab and people have car accidents and they go back in the Olympics."

We were interested in whether she was in pain or not and all I could do was talk to the medical people, who said she was probably in significant discomfort at times because being bedridden is not comfortable. She would wince and make noises when she was moved, so I suspect there was a lot of pain attached to that. I would say the whole business was ugly. I don't think burn victims have much fun, I don't think people who are in bad car accidents have much fun and I don't think my mother was really having a great time either. On the other hand, the doctors would say that when she wasn't being moved and they weren't doing anything to her, she probably wasn't in any great discomfort. But they were just guessing.

Then the next step was how do you find out what's there, because to me there are the questions of is this person suffering or not, and what does quality of life mean? But then the other question is, is this person who she was?—when you go further and you say if this person is in a vegetative state, is that really a human condition? Or is that more of an animal state?

So they wired her all up and asked her questions. The results came back and she scored something like in the fiftieth percentile. I said, "What does that mean?" They said, "It means she's definitely in there. She's definitely responsive to these tests. She might have gone in and out of focus, which means she got all the questions right when she was conscious and she didn't get any of them right when her brain went to sleep. Or she just got some. But some people score zero on this test and she scored in the fiftieth percentile. "So they believed she was in there. He was saying, "There's something going on in there." And this was after having psychiatrists and others say that she was in a vegetative state.

We found out the results at the beginning of August. The next weekend I got a call from my brother about my father: "You might want to come down."

My father had been on a slide from Christmas to August that accelerated. At the end, his bones were like coral, he was all stoked up on morphine, he had a lot of pain. It wasn't much of a life. He'd get up and get dressed every day, move around the house a bit. I called him on Friday and he was really happy; he didn't drink, but he was like he'd had a couple of gins. He said to me, "Do you think I'm kicking the bucket?" I said, "What do you mean?" And he gave a couple of analogies from the war. He was in the air force for England during the war. I said, "I don't know, but I know that at some point you will die." And he just spoke like he was punch-drunk almost. And we found that the last thing he'd done that night was write a bunch of cheques to pay for various things. But instead of writing a cheque out to Molly Maid, he'd written it out to Pretty Maids. It was sweet. His handwriting was not his handwriting, it was sort of slurred.

He didn't wake up the next morning. He stayed in a subconscious state, which is why my brother called me. After I flew down, he came out of it at one point and became conscious and he was trying to get out of bed but saying he really wanted to go to bed. I was holding on to him and he had this unbelievable strength and I said, "Do you want me to help you?" And he said, "Oh, bugger it. Bugger *you*." He was just violently mad, which was fantastic to see. But, of course, he was dead within a day.

We believe very strongly that no one deserves to die alone. Conversation lasts long after everything else goes. People who are almost dead can still hear you because people who come back from being almost dead say, "I couldn't move anything, I couldn't see, but I could hear your voices. I could hear you talking to me." So we talked to him. I held his hand and talked to him and read him Dylan Thomas—not that he cared for poetry, but I did it because I had a book with me at the time. My brother and I would talk about stuff. This was in my childhood bedroom, which was his bedroom then.

I felt my brother and I were involved in my father's death. The minister had come and given him his last rites. The doctors had said this is what's going to happen. There were no surprises. The nurses were very inclusive. They said, "He's on a drip right now, but if he shows any pain, take one of these vials and put it in here and you squirt it in there. If you give him a little bit more, he'll stay not conscious and it's at the end." My brother and I were actually taking the syringe with the morphine and putting it into the butterfly that was going into his vein and squirting it in. So, in a way, my brother and I accelerated the process by jacking up the morphine.

I don't want you to get the wrong idea. It wasn't like they said, "Here's the morphine that should last the month" and we juiced him up on the first night. It's not like they said give him a Scotch and we gave him six 40-ouncers. It wasn't like that. It was like they said, "Give him a Scotch every four hours, but you can give him as much as one every hour." So we just gave him one every hour. We just gave him the upper limit of what they recommended.

We watched his fingers go grey and cold. So there he was breathing and he got these completely grey, cold legs and then all of sudden they started to warm up again and they started to become pink and he got all the colour back in his fingertips and then it receded again. Death was happening. And then, at the end, there was this last breath.

The day after my father died, my brother, my sister and I went to my mother's bedside at the hospital to tell her, somehow, that her husband had died. And how do you do this? It's like trying to talk to a newborn baby: "Hi. I'm your dad, I'll be living upstairs for the next twenty years." So we stood in front of Mum and I guess I took the lead and I started by backing into it. I said, "Hi, Mum, I'm here with Bobby and Sarah," and they both said, "Hi, Mum," even though she was looking over our shoulder or past us—or maybe through us. And I said, "I want you to know that we just got the test back from Halifax and the doctors said that you're absolutely in there."

She looked at me and said, "How's Daddy?"

I hadn't heard her voice in four months and she said, "How's Daddy?" I was floored. I said, "Well, actually, he loved you very, very much and sorry to tell you that he died yesterday."

And then she said, "He's dead."

So, four words: "How's Daddy?" and "He's dead." And this is someone who's in a vegetative state? She wouldn't have said, "How's Daddy?" to the doctors or the nurses. She would have said, "How's John?" So she knew who she was talking to and she knew the context. It was gripping and awful.

When I talked to the doctors about it, they said she was still in a vegetative state. It's like everything is fried up there, but there are these little pathways in the brain and something linked with something and that worked. They basically said to me, "Don't think this means much. Don't think that she's fully functional and trapped inside."

The only analogy I can think of is you've taken your computer off your desk, dunked it in your bathtub, brought it out, dried it off and plugged it in. And you're just waiting for it to click into life, and that's what we did with my mum. We were like, "Okay, the pneumonia is gone, the meningitis is gone, your body is completely mangled, and that's just awful, but maybe you're in there and everything's going."

At my father's funeral the next week, I was quite concerned about getting videotape, which I'd never do for myself, but just in case my mother became more conscious she could see it if she needed closure. I went back afterward and told her all about it. We all treated her the whole time like she was herself, only trapped. But in a way I was hoping she was fried, because that kind of existence would be like being buried alive. It would be just dreadful.

We contrived to bring my mother home for Christmas. It was a huge SWAT team effort, but there she was, all dressed, in a wheelchair, sitting at the dining room table for a family dinner and sitting in the living room while we opened presents. And it was either the most perverse charade or a very beautiful, beautiful gesture. Even if she only surfaced for a few seconds, it was her world, her environment.

My sister sensed that Mum was happy to be there, but I can't emphasize enough how detached she was, in the sense she was sitting there just looking around like ... [he demonstrated the slow movement of vacant eyes]. When I went to leave at six in the morning—the car was loaded, the kids were in the car and I had to race to Halifax to get an airplane that was leaving in no time—I went in to say goodbye and I leaned down and I hugged her. She was lying there and I said, "I love you, I love you so much. I really love you."

And she said, "I love you."

Now, it's a conditioned response that when someone says "I love you," you say "I love you" back. But for me it was real and she was there, and I feel desperate about the fact that I left while she was conscious, because she said "I love you" in the same way she'd said it for years. And I don't need to analyze that.

I had these crazy ideas that I was going to put my mother somewhere. I went to a nursing home and I picked up the forms to fill out. I felt this huge anxiety because I'd promised my mother she would never go to a nursing home. I never thought this would happen. I just thought, "Worse case, we mortgage the house until it's over. We just spend every nickel that my parents had, taking care of them."

I had this idea that I could turn the house into a hospice. All I needed to do was find another broken-down old creature to stuff in the room down the hall and we could share the medical care. I had this whole idea that I was going to do everything to keep her in her house with some level of a life. It was a stretch, but I was prepared to believe that it was worth supporting that.

But then we started talking about it and it didn't take very long to figure out it was an extremely ghoulish approach and that my mother would not have accepted those terms. My mother was seventy-eight and she was not going to get better. It wasn't like she was twenty-five and might get her physical capabilities back. She was on the long end of life. She couldn't communicate and she couldn't experience. Maybe she was only conscious a minute a month. And if she was conscious more than that, what's the overlap of me saying "I love you" and her saying "I love you" back at the right moment compared to what she had as a life—being in her garden, being in her house, going downtown to do a little shopping, being with my dad, talking to us on the phone every few days, writing us a letter, us turning up once a month or whatever?

After Christmas, we had the conversation about ending her life. Because this was no life. With living wills, some people would say, "If I can't walk upstairs to my own bed, I want my life over." But you talk to quadriplegics and they are happy. Somehow they've found a way to be happy about what their life is. Some people would say, "If I'm blind, then I'm done." But then you find out that that's not true. We cling to life unbelievably.

So if you're facing the question do you end somebody's life, how do you possibly get to where they are? We never had any sense of my mother's wishes except that she'd never liked being sick and had never been sick—had only really ever been in a hospital bed to have kids. If we had been able to ask her, she would have said she didn't want to be alive. We never had that conversation, but if you went to your parents' house and you were thirsty and you didn't ask but you went into the kitchen and you poured yourself a glass of water, would your mother have let you have that water? That's about as close as I can get to answering it. She would not have accepted that life. Not being able to move her limbs and hold her children, that's just what you take, but I think she would not have accepted her brain not working.

So we started talking about it and the fact there wasn't going to be any change, she was not going to get better. There was no endgame that's recognizable as being worthwhile on our terms or on her terms. So what's the opposite? She shouldn't be alive. It should be over. It would have been better for everybody if she'd died of pneumonia the first month she was in there. All that superhuman effort to keep her alive was misguided because the promise of her being herself or having her life back was over.

So had we prepared for our mother's death? Yes. We had a lot of time to deal with that, from April to February. Had we made a decision that nobody—the doctors, the nurses, us, my mother's friends, my mother's family, nobody—wanted her to be alive another minute? There was nothing in it for anybody. But I cried for weeks at the beginning. It was desperate. It's only in hindsight that I came to terms with the fact that most people's parents die before them. A lot of people don't die well. Few people have an attractive death, an appealing, comfortable, attractive death. It's often not so great. My mother was fried, and a lot of people die of awful things, and that's what happens and this is just how she died. So stop thinking you're unique.

We talked to the doctors and they were all completely supportive. Nobody thought her life was worth living or that she was even there. And we talked about how to do it and basically it was explained to me by those doctors and others that when you take someone off life support—which, for her, meant taking out the feeding tube—it was not a painful process.

But then there's the execution of it. I still have a hard time thinking about starving someone to death. We were told it could be three or four weeks. That the feeding tube comes out and she'd be hungry, but it's not a significant thing. She'd be thirsty, but then that goes away. But does it? It all sounds awful to me. At the point where they pulled the feeding tube out, if they'd been able to treat my mother like they put your pet to sleep at the vet? Absolutely. I would have been very happy to do that. Maybe they could have a twenty-four-hour period when there's no feeding tube and you can put wet cloths on her forehead.

Instead, my brother and I went days with no sleep, completely implicated in the process. But, actually, we thought it was less cowardly to be active. My mother had struggled for ten months with this degrading, painful existence. At the end, do you pull a tube out and wait? There's nothing natural about

her state, her condition, her hopes, her chances. It's a totally
contrived existence. She's been completely propped up for ten
months, so why do we at the end shift it over to let God take
what God will take?

We made a decision as a family that this should be over. We
talked about it and we talked to the doctor and we all wanted it
to happen. We discussed it and discussed it and discussed it and
we all signed it. My brother, my sister and I were a hundred
percent committed to the idea of ending our mother's life. My
sister was saying maybe we should bring her home for a month
and then do it. But why? If we've reached the point where we've
made a decision that we're done with all the experiments and
all the hope, let's end this. There was no pre-grieving to be
done, there was no further analysis to be done, there was no
second-guessing to be done.

The minister who gave last rites to my father was a friend of
my dad's. He came by as a family friend and we all held hands
and he said a prayer and talked about stuff. It wasn't necessarily
a religious moment as much as galvanizing love.

The doctors took the feeding tube out. My brother and I
were there with our mother, around the clock. I think going
through it with my father prepared me for dealing with my
mother. We gave her water, we kept her hydrated because that
was a comfort thing, and we administered morphine. They
would come in, give her morphine and then we would give it
to her. And we would ask for more. Basically, there was this
tacit arrangement where they prescribed a certain amount of
morphine every hour for, I guess, the pain of having your
feeding tube removed. And we had it jumped up by saying, "I
think she's in pain." So they would call the doctor and come
in and give us morphine and we would squirt it into the
butterfly.

For the first day, we were on course. And on the second day, we accelerated it a bit and on the third day we accelerated it a bit more. With my father it was very benign, whereas with my mother it was very active. It was an aggressive course. We weren't running down to the drawer and stealing all the morphine and juicing my mum up, but they'd said to us, "We're going to give this amount to your mother every two hours, but we can do it more often if there's any distress."

It takes three or four weeks for someone to die of starvation and with my brother and I doing this, it took five days. [He let out a huge sigh.]

I don't know if the medical team was in favour of this, but they were supportive of the idea of taking out the feeding tube. They didn't say no to more morphine and they didn't say you're pushing the limits. They were aware of how much morphine my mother got, but they were still going through the whole charade of turning her every half-hour. When she was having difficulty breathing, they put a mask on her. I was like, Jesus, you know, what are we doing? She's so, so stoned. She's so not here, so what if she's having trouble breathing? At the end, she went through the same process that my father did of the shallow breathing.

It was actually quite a beautiful thing to witness, to be involved with.

3 The Michelangelo Principle
Clinical ethicists and the conflict of "shoulds"

AS KERRY BOWMAN walked into the fifteenth-floor classroom for noon rounds, he knew he was probably about to face a tough crowd. He's learned the hard way that medical residents, like the doctors they will soon become, can have a "Why are you telling me this?" attitude, as if all this talk about ethics was just common sense or somehow beneath them. One of Bowman's tasks as Mount Sinai Hospital's clinical ethicist is to train staff on various ethical matters, and this particular summer he was working his way through sessions on informed consent. Although the hospital had received a good rating from an international accreditation body, it had been found wanting on informed consent, so over eighteen months Bowman met with the entire medical staff to go over it with them. The medical community uses the term "informed consent" to talk about patients and their families making decisions based on knowing and understanding the risks and benefits of an operation, procedure or other treatment as well as the potential consequences of not getting that care. The laws in Canada regarding informed consent have changed a great deal over the years, but Bowman was worried that our approach was still forty years behind where it should be.

Training the entire staff is no easy task, especially in a teaching hospital where there's so much turnover. And there are different attitudes to learning about ethics to contend with: nurses, for example, are invariably engaged and keen to debate the issues, but doctors can be a challenge. As Bowman went through his final preparations, one or two people walked into the room, glanced at the title slide on the screen, grabbed a wrap and a pop and promptly left. Though the number did fluctuate during the lecture, about ten residents stayed—most sitting around a long conference table—and only a couple had glazed eyes. Dressed casually in khakis and a short-sleeved shirt, Bowman began by whipping through a series of questions and answers in a PowerPoint presentation. Then he illustrated his argument with a case that ended in a lawsuit after doctors thought they had received informed consent from a patient. The doctors had used the man's son as the translator and what they didn't know was that the son hadn't given his father complete translations for fear of upsetting him.

Even when patients speak English, there can be breakdowns in communication. The advantage of being treated in a teaching hospital such as Mount Sinai is that there are plenty of talented, accomplished medical people there and the standard of care tends to be as contemporary as it gets. But there are also many young people who don't stick around because they rotate from hospital to hospital. And that can result in poor communication. When family members complain, "Everyone is telling us something different," they're usually right.

Aside from the institutional problems, too many people in medicine just don't know how to talk to people. One doctor told a family, "You must remain cognizant of three clinical issues." When Bowman suggested the family wouldn't understand "cognizant" or "clinical issues," the doctor—"a very learned man"—disagreed. But the general population isn't nearly as educated as doctors are. That's why most newspapers aim to be understood by people who read only at a grade-school level. So doctors and nurses need to work at using understandable language. "People say to me that medicine is not a popularity contest," Bowman told the residents, "but social skills are enormously important."

Still, no matter how gregarious doctors are, they will run into trying situations. And the trickiest issue in the tricky world of consent can be the Do Not Resuscitate (DNR) order. DNRs instruct medical personnel not to perform cardiopulmonary resuscitation on a patient whose heart or breathing has stopped. If a woman's heart stops, the medical team can do everything possible either to save her or let her die peacefully, but she should decide in advance just how far to go—or, if she can't, her family should.

For many sons and daughters, the initial instinct is to say, "Yes, of course, save my mother." Most of them think of CPR as what they learned in first aid or have seen on television: mouth-to-mouth resuscitation or external chest compression. But advanced CPR can include electric shock, inserting a tube into the airway or injecting medication into the heart. And the sad truth is that most old or seriously ill people don't do well after being revived. Just pumping on the chest to get the heart going can mean broken ribs. Once a doctor explains that, many people agree that a DNR order might not be such a bad idea.

Still, DNRs are controversial, especially when doctors impose them on their own —and sometimes even result in legal battles. In 1998, Andrew Sawatzky was not a well man. The seventy-nine-year-old had Parkinson's, pneumonia and dementia; he'd also suffered several strokes. He couldn't talk, had trouble swallowing and breathed through a tube in his windpipe. After several months, his doctors at Winnipeg's Riverside Health Centre slapped a DNR order on his chart. They'd approached his wife, Helene, about it before and she'd refused. When she found out the doctors had ignored her wishes, she went to court. After hearing both sides, the judge stated that the case dealt with fundamental questions about a patient's right to medical treatment and a doctor's obligation to provide it. "Those questions raise serious legal, moral, ethical, medical and practical issues on which there is unlikely to ever be complete agreement," reasoned the judge. "I think that many Canadians have been surprised to learn that a doctor can make a 'do not resuscitate' order without the consent of a patient or his or her family, yet that appears to be the current state of the law in Canada, Britain and the United States." The judge granted a temporary injunction lifting the DNR order and instructed the two sides to try to work it out. But Sawatzky transferred out of Riverside Health Centre and later died, so there was never a final ruling in the case. And that meant the legality of unilateral DNRs remained unclear.

Most cases don't end up in the courts, of course, but as a clinical ethicist, Bowman often mediates such disputes. Since everyone knows about the financial pressure on our health care system, some families may see a doctor recommending a DNR order as a cost-saving move rather than something to preserve the patient's quality of life. "The worst thing to do is to huff and puff and get into a power struggle," he advised the medical residents, "because that's when the family digs in."

None of the doctors-in-training in the room took notes, and when Bowman asked for questions or comments, only one or two people spoke up. They did listen politely and, apparently, attentively—but even when Bowman suggested that not getting proper informed consent on a DNR order could mean ending up on the front page of the *Toronto Sun*, they didn't react much.

Finally, he assured everyone that he was always available if any of them ever ran into any ethical dilemmas. But the vibe in the room was that doctors are too busy and events in hospitals happen too quickly: decisions must be made immediately, so there's no time to hold lofty ethical debates.

At five minutes before one o'clock, everyone cleared out Later, Bowman, who admitted he'd seen worse, including complete silence or a roomful of unspoken resistance, joked, "Well, at least they weren't sleeping."

A CLINICAL ETHICIST may seem a bore or a waste of time to overworked and under-experienced medical residents, but for the public, even the idea of someone being employed as an ethicist can be baffling. I asked Linda Wright, the bioethicist at the University Health Network (UNH), which consists of the Toronto General, Toronto Western and Princess Margaret hospitals, how she explains to the general public what she does. "It's very difficult, actually," she said, pointing out that not every nurse or social worker knows, so it's not surprising that others don't either. "What I try to explain is we get involved whenever there's that part of us that isn't sure what the right thing to do is, so whenever there's a clash of values. Some of our values say we should keep this person alive because that's the only humane thing to do, and the other part of us says we should let this person die in peace and not assault their body with all this equipment and interventions."

For families, this conflict of "shoulds" can make dealing with death all the more painful and difficult. But it can also take its toll on hospital staff and lead to burnout and people quitting their jobs if it isn't addressed. A career in health care can mean being a party to a lot of tough decisions—including withdrawing treatment from dying patients and terminating pregnancies for genetic reasons—that can lead to emotional distress. Some choices will make doctors and nurses feel bad even when they believe they're doing the right thing. So a Linda Wright or a Kerry Bowman will get together with nurses, for example, to discuss not just what judgments were made, but how they were made. Bowman is convinced people feel better after an ethics seminar: "We really shine the light of day on some of the more painful areas of what we have to face in medicine. Now, you can say this is shallow pap and it's no different than the feel-good crap on TV, but I try not to talk very much. It's dialogue and there's no great speech."

When I wondered why we need ethicists now when we didn't before, Wright at first said, "Maybe we did before and didn't recognize it." But then she explained that not only has the explosion in medical technology generated a lot of tough questions for us, so have changes in society's attitudes. Originally, doctors performed kidney transplants only between siblings or parents and children, but now it's been done between donors and recipients who've met over the internet. "People challenged us and wouldn't take no for an answer and made us stop and think and reflect," said Wright, who specializes in transplant ethics. "We had to look at what we were doing and why we were doing it."

The rise of activism in the sixties—including a much greater sense of consumers' rights—meant people were more likely to question everything and everybody, including doctors. For a while, as respect for experts began to decline in the 1960s and '70s, doctors managed to maintain at least some of their high standing. (Indeed, if two doctors—invariably men in those days—walked into an elevator, nurses—invariably women— were expected to step out and wait for the next one.) But it couldn't last, especially as the public became better educated and had easier access to information. The spread of AIDS starting in the eighties may have been the turning point as activists began to collect and distribute the information that AIDS patients wanted but couldn't get from their doctors. Instead of being content to be the subject of the process, the patients began to take some control and demanded to be part of it. After that, the breast cancer community used many of the same tactics. And now, with widespread use of the internet, sharing information and building communities is easier than ever. Sangeeta Mehta, an ICU doctor and respirologist at Mount Sinai who finished med school in 1990, doesn't regret the passing of the days when doctors held such unquestioned sway. "I think this is a better time, and breast cancer patients and AIDS patients needed to advocate for themselves and it's led to dramatic increases in research and funding in those areas," she said. But like many in her profession, she worries that too often the information people glean from the internet or from friends is misleading—and that even when it's right, it can lack context. "They cling to that and often their expectations of what's going to happen conflict with what we're telling them."

Adding to the sometimes unrealistic expectations of patients, financial pressure on our health care system has increased, complicating the jobs of doctors, nurses and bioethicists even further. The dilemma becomes not just over whether we should hook this patient up to that machine or continue to give him that treatment, but also if can we afford it. So we have resource allocation that we didn't have before. "The *Canada Health Act* was developed in a time of plenty," noted Wright. "And now suddenly we're forced to say we don't have enough money for all of these things."

Conflict can also sometimes arise because medical professionals tend to speak in language that many people find off-putting, even when they can understand it. For one thing, many doctors aren't into sugar-coating the truth. "We're a pretty blunt group, and if we don't think someone is going to survive, we tell the patient's family," admitted Mehta. A doctor might, for example, advise a family, "Based on my experience with the last several patients like this, he won't make it out of the ICU." But sometimes families don't care about the odds. And sometimes they just don't trust the medical team.

After nearly two decades in and around ICUs, first as a social worker and then as an ethicist, Bowman knows more about medicine than he often lets on, though he doesn't use medical jargon when speaking to families and never says, "In my medical opinion..." But even more dangerous than jargon, according to Bowman, are some of the loaded statements doctors and nurses make to families in end-of-life situations. Lines such as, "We're no longer extending her life, we're delaying her death" or "If it were my father, I would do this." While some people may be tempted to see such statements as a way of bonding with the family, Bowman disagrees. "It's not their father, it's someone else's father. And people aren't the same, families aren't the same, cultures aren't the same. But the value-laden language just flies around."

Most doctors and nurses have had no formal training in conflict resolution and it's easy for them to become victims of their medical backgrounds. Some really believe that if they can just explain the situation in words the family can understand, there will be this moment of comprehension, as if the family just hadn't understood all those other times. "For some people, it is going to work, but the first time, or the second, not the twenty-fifth," said Bowman. "I'm not exaggerating when I say twenty-five times, and I'm talking everybody from the person who sweeps the floor practically to the head of surgery having a go at them. It pisses them off. It's not a good way to handle these things."

Despite his concern that some health care workers are too quick to accuse family members of being in denial as soon as they have the audacity to challenge one of their recommendations, he also appreciates how hard doctors and nurses work. And his job is not just about what he can do for patients and their families; he's also there to help health care workers. Most of them, he's convinced, are good people who care and have a social conscience—after all, there are a lot of easier jobs, ones that pay more and don't have the crushing hours. But he also knows that sometimes people haven't thought deeply about some long-held practices they've just taken for granted. That changes once Bowman convinces them to consider the questions they haven't been asking themselves. "People's appetite for ethics is quite strong. It's a consciousness-raising thing—I've seen it in myself and I've seen it in people I've taught."

PERHAPS THE BEST PLACE to view a proliferation of professionals is at an industry conference, so I drove down to Montreal for the annual gathering of the Canadian Bioethics Society. For the first time, the CBS and the American Society for Bioethics and Humanities had hooked up to hold a joint meeting, which meant the conference was a lot larger than usual. (When the two groups first started talking about doing a joint meeting, the Americans said they were up for it, but only if Montreal was the host city. I can't say I blame them.)

The theme of the conference was "Bioethics Across Borders" and included panel sessions with riveting titles such as "Genomics and Pluralism in Canada: Discussions to Deepen Dialogue" and "Benchside Consultation: Developing a New Paradigm for Integrating Ethics and Biomedical Research." Obviously, it was no place for regular folk, especially since the presenters ranged from those with slick PowerPoint presentations to some who simply read their academic papers. But close to nine hundred people from both countries were interested enough to register for the conference, and most of the panel and paper sessions were well attended. The mood was serious and nerdy.

Inside the small press room, which featured decor no sane person would ever select—various uninspiring shades of brown in the rug and on the walls—there was a round table in the middle and rectangular tables along the wall. Those tables held none of the bumpf (press kits, bios, news releases) reporters normally find at such events. And while a few science journalists did attend, there weren't many.

Nuala Kenny, a nun, pediatrician with a special interest in the care of dying children, former deputy minister of health and founder of Dalhousie University's Department of Bioethics, gave an energetic, funny and no-nonsense keynote speech. Later that day, we met in the press room and ignored the rhubarb from the crowd outside. "Up until the sixties, docs made the decisions," she explained to me. Patients assumed doctor knew best, but then the decisions grew more complicated and the world more pluralist. In a country as diverse as Canada, such clashes seem inevitable since even when an Orthodox Jewish doctor treats an Orthodox Jewish patient, they might not agree. "We can no longer assume that an individual doctor's view of the right and good and an individual patient's are consistent. So modern bioethics comes into play here to say there are other perspectives and other ways of understanding good."

Though her interest in ethics is informed by her religious beliefs, Kenny can offer several perspectives, since she's not just a nun but someone with experience as a doctor, an administrator and a teacher. "The nature of bioethics is interdisciplinary," she noted. "The more perspectives that we have on the right and the good in a given case, the better." Still, Kenny's not blind to the downside of people from many backgrounds—including religion, philosophy, medicine, law, social work and hospital administration—treating ethics like it's the latest hot job craze. The danger is that anyone who's ever sat on one bioethics committee or read one book may claim to be a bioethicist. "Because we do it from many perspectives there can be the absence of core rigorous knowledge."

KENNY IS A SOLIDLY BUILT WOMAN with a rectangular face, a ruddy complexion, bright eyes and an easy smile. A passionate and direct speaker, she used her hands a lot to punctuate her strong opinions, even when the subject veered into the theoretical. "To know your stuff in medicine is really important, to have good technical skills is really important, but you're not a good doctor in the fullest sense of the tradition unless you have some understanding of the moral nature of illness for patients and their loved ones," she said. One more elderly man in an emergency room with a heart attack may be routine for a doctor but not for his wife or children. "It's not excellence in medicine until you understand these other dimensions."

While some doctors and nurses see the clinical ethicist as someone who shares their perspective and can explain it to patients and families as an independent third party, that doesn't mean the ethicist always takes their side. "Sometimes, and not rarely, you get an ethics consult for the sole reason that they want you to agree with them and they have no doubt you will," Kerry Bowman told me. He will meet with doctors who want him to see that the family is nuts and asking for ludicrous things and that it's unethical, because they can't have an eighty-five-year-old blocking a bed when nineteen-year-olds are in Emerg. Based on their view of common sense, doctors often expect ethicists to agree with them at once. But Bowman has a knack for sensing when things aren't as straightforward as they appear—or as doctors might present them.

Other times, he must overcome the fear, from both sides, that he will walk in, listen to a situation and announce, "I have this equation, this application of philosophical logic that's essentially like a mathematical equation—and you're right and you're wrong." That's exactly what a good clinical ethicist avoids doing, preferring to try to illuminate the issues, consider the options and help the best answer emerge from the discussion. To be a successful mediator, especially one with the ability to coax out all the ethical threads in a case, he must navigate competing ideas, principles and goals.

That approach inevitably means some doctors view Bowman, who has a Ph.D. in bioethics but is not a medical doctor, with disdain. Their argument usually goes: "I'm incredibly busy, I bring in a difficult situation to this so-called ethicist, we spend forty minutes talking about one side, the other side, this issue, that issue, and he doesn't make any solid recommendation. What an enormous waste of time."

While trying to avoid seeming pointless to the doctors, Bowman must sometimes also work hard to win the trust of the family members so they don't see him as simply another employee of the hospital they are battling with—though not being a member of the medical team helps. Some families may see him as an advocate, but others may look to him for answers, and that can lead to accusations that he has too much power. "I don't know how to gauge my influence," said Bowman hesitantly. He believes his job is to let the answers rise to the surface on their own, but he knows it's not always that simple. "I'd be foolish to say my values have no influence over anything. I strive to be as objective as possible, but you can't fully control these things. So there is always some influence exerted."

That may be inevitable, but doctors also exert considerable influence on patients and their families. The end of a loved one's life is, needless to say, a profoundly emotional experience. And yet far too often case conferences (the meetings between the medical team and the family to discuss what to do) open with a doctor giving a long technical explanation in impenetrable jargon—or, as Bowman characterizes it, "eighteen minutes of wah-wah-wah." Meanwhile, the family members are so anxious they can barely hear. It is not the beginning of a beautiful relationship. And it often grows worse because doctors like to get their way.

Several times during the many discussions I have had with him over the years, Bowman—whose mother is alive and well but whose father dropped dead of a heart attack twenty years ago—has mentioned, in unflattering terms, the work of Elizabeth Kubler-Ross, the psychiatrist and author who wrote *On Death and Dying*, a 1969 book that popularized the notion that people approaching death experience five emotions: denial, anger, bargaining, depression and acceptance. Despite earning Bowman's condemnation as "bad theory, bad research, bad book," Kubler-Ross's work has garnered so many believers that *The Simpsons* skillfully satirized it in a delightful episode called "One Fish, Two Fish, Blowfish, Blue Fish." After eating improperly prepared blowfish, Homer Simpson visits his doctor, Julius Hibbert, and learns he has twenty-four hours to live—actually twenty-two, because he spent so long in the waiting room (a sly dig in itself, though one that probably has even more resonance in Canada than in the United States). Dr. Hibbert explains the five stages Homer can expect to go through, the first of which is denial.

HOMER: No way! Because I'm not dying!
DR. HIBBERT: The second is anger.
HOMER, MOVING THREATENINGLY TOWARD THE DOCTOR: Why you little … !

DR. HIBBERT: After that comes fear.

HOMER, COWERING: What's after fear? What's after fear?

DR. HIBBERT: Bargaining.

HOMER : Doc, you gotta get me out of this! I'll make it worth your while!

DR. HIBBERT: Finally, acceptance.

HOMER: Well, we all gotta go sometime.

DR. HIBBERT: Mr. Simpson, your progress astounds me.

To the writers behind the animated show, Kubler-Ross's five stages (which they didn't get quite right) were just fodder for their subversive humour, but the scene also skewers—perhaps unwittingly—the medical profession, since too often doctors really would like to see patients and their families progress to acceptance just that quickly. And when they don't, doctors and nurses often dismiss them as being stuck in denial. That's when medical teams call in the clinical ethicist, hoping a third party can help unstick them.

STAN, A SUCCESSFUL fifty-eight-year-old businessman, had a major brain-stem stroke while playing tennis. He quickly went from Emerg to the ICU, where he survived on a ventilator. Because he showed no neurological responses of any significance, the next day the doctors, believing there was nothing left of this man, recommended a "one-way wean."

"It means pulling the plug," Bowman whispered when I repeated the jargon quizzically. In order to take someone off a ventilator, doctors reduce the settings and slowly force the patient to use his or her lungs again. Under ideal circumstances, weaning a person from a ventilator is a crucial part of the recovery. But sometimes recovery is not possible. "A one-way wean," Bowman explained, "is a medical term—I don't like it, but it's what's used—that means you don't put them back on if it fails. And you're expecting them to fail, so it's sort of a disingenuous term if you ask me."

Stan's three oldest children and his second wife believed he wouldn't want to continue living in a vegetative state and they wanted to respect his wishes as they understood them. Although he'd never said, "If I end up like this, pull the plug," they were interpreting his values, as family members often have to do in such situations. Letting him go seemed the right thing to do, so they were in favour of accepting the medical team's recommendation to withdraw treatment. But one daughter, the youngest by ten years, thought everybody was rushing into this after having only just heard the doctors' advice and the rest of her family backed off a bit. This created a little friction between the daughter and the rest of her family, but much more between the medical team and the daughter.

Later that same day, the medical team called Bowman to say they had a daughter in denial. That's how his referrals usually begin: a doctor phones with some problem, generally tension or a controversy. Bowman reads the charts first, talks to the medical team and then he meets with the family. As he follows the situation, he'll often meet the family members once or twice a day and sit in on—or even chair—case conferences. And he'll meet with the doctors to talk about any developments. If the patient is dying, he might sit with the family and go through it with them. He also tells family members to give him a call if they're upset or things are going badly or they have new information or they want to review something. And he will often check on people to see how they're doing. He typically has one to three cases on the go at any given time, and if he's following an end-of-life dilemma he'll usually devote at least a couple of hours a day to it. "The thing is, once you start, you really have to hang in; you can't just say, 'Aw, I'm too busy, I'm not coming in today.'"

As Bowman began negotiating between Stan's family and the team, he recommended slowing things down, because the youngest daughter wasn't ready and it might put a permanent strain on the family. This could have been almost routine for Bowman except that the family soon realized that while Stan couldn't speak or move, his mind was fine. He was trapped in a body that couldn't do anything except blink in response to questions. He was "locked in."

Initially, his wife and children communicated with him by asking yes-or-no questions, but he also started to be able to spell out words. (This is not unheard of. In 1995, Jean-Dominique Bauby, a forty-two-year-old French journalist and the editor of *Elle* magazine, suffered a brain-stem stroke that left him in a coma for twenty days. When he resurfaced, he discovered the only part of his body he could use was his left eyelid. He communicated by blinking to indicate the letter he wanted as someone ran through the alphabet. Eventually he became so adept at it that he wrote a short but moving memoir called *The Diving Bell and the Butterfly*. It came out in 1997, two days before Bauby died, and in 2007 director Julian Schnabel turned the book into a visually stunning film.)

Once Stan was able to have a "conversation" with his family, he made it clear that they were rushing things a bit. He didn't want to carry on in that state indefinitely, but he did want to say goodbye to people. Over the next few days, he was able to spend some time with his family and friends. (On the other hand, he also had to contend with an ex-wife. "Everybody shows up in these situations," said Bowman. "Imagine being locked in and having to listen to your ex-wife. My God. Poor guy, I really felt for him, but she slipped through the net. She was on about stuff that happened in the seventies. Anyway, we ushered her out.")

Six days after his stroke, Stan was ready for his final goodbye.

Bowman sees the case as a reminder that the system can sometimes move too fast, even when there's a potential misdiagnosis. Worse, he worries about how quick doctors and nurses are to dismiss dissenters as irrational. "You had one daughter who was labelled by some of the staff as being 'in denial,' 'resistant,' as having 'her own issues,'" said Bowman, noting that, in fact, she turned out to be the one who was most in touch. "I get referrals endlessly about people in denial, but grieving or anticipated grieving, whatever you want to call it—preparing for someone's death—is a process and we're not all the same. Some people come to terms with this very quickly and some people don't."

THOUGH LINDA WRIGHT has lived in Canada since the mid-seventies, she hasn't lost all of the lovely Irish lilt in her voice. Growing up a Protestant with Catholic relatives in Belfast, she watched the hatred in Northern Ireland with dismay. As she told me about living through the Troubles, her blue eyes welled up with tears, and when she blew her nose, a tear fell from her cheek onto her dark blue pantsuit. A social worker in south Belfast, she grew frustrated at being unable to go out at night and enjoy life because of the sectarian violence, so she left for Atlantic City, where she worked as a waitress before travelling around North America. Out of money, she went home to Belfast and saved up so she could return. Ending up in Montreal, a city going through its own us-versus-them convulsions, she once again found the strife painful to watch, but it helped her growing ability to see issues from more than one side. "Part of me," she explained, "was always an observer in life, as much as being a participant."

After moving to Toronto with her husband, and armed with a master's in social work from McGill, she worked in the transplant unit at the University Health Network and became interested in bioethics. What she learned as a social worker—including communication skills and interviewing techniques—has helped her as a clinical ethicist. By asking probing, open-ended questions and quickly putting people at ease ("You practise getting into the other person's shoes if you can"), Wright can often lead patients to tell her what no one else could cajole out of them. "How do you get all this stuff?" doctors and nurses often ask her. "He didn't tell me any of that."

But gleaning information no one else can elicit is only the start. Television shows such as *ER* always make ethical dilemmas look easy. The predicaments are often based on real cases, but the resolutions are ridiculously simplistic. "What tends to happen," Kerry Bowman said to me, "is the person who gives the most eloquent speech—which is usually at about fifty-four minutes— silences everybody. The penny drops and everybody realizes there's the truth and it's solved. In real life, it's not like that."

In real life, fed-up doctors and nurses complain: "This family is nuts. They have personality disorders. They're threatening. They're abusive." Meanwhile, appalled families protest: "They won't listen. All they want to do is save money. They have my father reduced to a hunk of meat. This is horrible. This is a violation of everything I believe in." The sides are far too entrenched for an eloquent speech to do much good.

Such disputes can quickly escalate in a hospital. "The greater the tension, the more time it eats. It just gets bigger and bigger and bigger, so a problem that was this big on Monday is this big on Friday," Bowman said, stretching his arms wide, then wider still. "The more you fight, the bigger it gets, and fighting is a terrible use of resources." That's why one of his goals is to increase the ethical understanding of everyone at Mount Sinai, especially the doctors. After all, aside from the desire to stay off the front page of the newspaper, hospitals would quickly go into organizational cardiac arrest if doctors had to call in the clinical ethicist every time there was a conflict.

And all good doctors should have a basic grasp of the ethical challenges they face. "It would be a real mistake to think that ethical medical practice turns on the clinical ethicist," said Peter Singer, who from 1995 to 2006 was the director of the University of Toronto's Joint Centre for Bioethics (JCB) while continuing to practise internal medicine for a month or two a year. "There is not a day that goes by where some ethical challenge doesn't present itself in the care of the patient." If a family asks him not to tell an elderly patient who is from a different culture that she has cancer, a doctor such as Singer, knowing he can't lie to a patient, will try to convince the family that it's a good idea to be honest, because the patient may know anyway, she has a right to know and she should have the opportunity to plan her affairs. If that doesn't work, Singer might suggest that he—with or without the family—talk to her in a way that gives her a chance to ask and learn about her illness. That may be enough if the patient needs no operation or other procedure, but if the medical situation requires something more, the doctor has to be more aggressive, because that takes it from the realm of truth telling into consent. But that approach is not some skill he developed because of the position he held at the JCB; in fact, Singer told me, all ethically competent doctors would do the same. "They shouldn't need a clinical ethics person to tell them that."

That's certainly Sangeeta Mehta's take. Since the doctor started working at Mount Sinai in 1997, she has benefited from Bowman's expertise on occasion, but she doesn't call him on a regular basis. "We're used to dealing with conflict, and when he's not around we deal with it," she said. "We would call Kerry in when it's really quite profound conflict."

Mehta did want Bowman's help for a case that involved a man in his fifties who came into the ICU with pneumonia. Mentally and physically disabled for most of his life, he could feed himself and dress himself, so he wasn't dependent on others for all of his care. He had muscular dystrophy and his three sisters had taken care of him for many years before they put him in the home. But he wasn't happy there, and grew quite depressed and deteriorated physically.

Since he had aspirated his food—it went into his lungs instead of his stomach—he was on a ventilator and had a tube down his throat to help him breathe. His sisters were extremely upset when they learned about these measures. He shouldn't be resuscitated, they said, and he shouldn't be kept alive. They wanted the doctors to pull the tube out and let him go. He couldn't speak because of the breathing tube, and his sisters said he was not competent to make decisions for himself anyway. At the same time, they also claimed that in the past he had asked that he not be maintained on life support indefinitely. But if the man was developmentally disabled, Mehta and the medical team wondered how he was able to express those wishes—or even understand what it meant to be on life support.

The concept of capacity is complicated. There was a time when a doctor or nurse would put questions to someone coming out of an operation or awakening from unconsciousness: "What's your mother's maiden name?" "What month is it?" Or even, "Who's the prime minister?" (One elderly man surfacing from a coma at Mount Sinai said, "Aw, who cares? It's always a Liberal.")

Patients who couldn't answer satisfactorily were not allowed to make health care decisions for themselves. But many experts thought this was a denial of rights to some people, including children, people with mental health histories and elderly people with early dementia. Someone with early dementia might have been highly functional but was losing the right to make health care decisions for herself because she couldn't remember what month it was. So the thinking changed, as did the legislation. Now anyone, regardless of age or mental history, who can fully understand his or her medical condition and the risks and benefits of any proposed treatment, has the capacity to make the decision.

Fortunately, Mehta's patient was alert and awake on the breathing machine, so the medical team could interact with him. And despite what the sisters had said, he seemed able to understand the nurses' directions and respond appropriately by nodding or shaking his head. So one of the nurses asked him, "Do you want us to take this tube out and let you die?"

When his answer was clearly no, Mehta decided to get Bowman involved. He met with the sisters and then—along with the doctor, as well as a nurse and a chaplain—he talked to the brother, who again made it clear that he didn't want to die. He also expressed that he wasn't so certain that his sisters loved him.

Bowman told the sisters that their brother wanted to live, and explained that the medical team and the hospital had an ethical obligation to respect his wishes. "They were quite angry," remembered Mehta. "But it supported our position, and legally it's always helpful to have people like Kerry involved as well."

Still, Bowman is not the only resource someone like Mehta can turn to in trying situations. Another difficult case involved a young woman who was dying of sarcoma and had written that she wanted to be taken off the breathing machine. Her husband, however, absolutely refused to let that happen and was angry at the medical team for even having conversations about it with her. Although his wife was clearly competent, he insisted she was too stressed to make such decisions. Mehta realized she couldn't go against his wishes because the death of his wife was something he'd have to live with the rest of his life. But she was unsure whether she should call in Bowman or someone from palliative care who could help the medical team manage both the physical and emotional symptoms and sit down with the husband and help him with the dying process. Mehta chose palliative care, and a few days later the patient changed her mind and said she wanted to keep fighting for her life. "I think we could have called Kerry in," Mehta said, "but we would have needed palliative care anyway."

WHEN CULTURAL DIFFERENCES exacerbate conflict, palliative care isn't enough. Dusana, a woman with advanced cancer eating away at her spine, arrived in the ICU after spine stabilization surgery. She was on a ventilator, didn't regain consciousness and began to deteriorate. Her skin started breaking down and gave off a bad odour. Nevertheless, her only child, Rachel, asked that everything be done to keep her mother alive.

The medical team was quick to label the thirty-six-year-old daughter. She was "locked in denial" and "too selfish to consider her own mother." She had "irrational expectations of the medical system" and "wants miracles when they can't be done." It got so bad that some nurses didn't want to be in the same room as Rachel, and a couple even began to say that on ethical grounds they didn't want to take care of Dusana any longer—this is normally less common with nurses than with doctors—because they felt it was wrong and that no child had the right to do that to anybody.

"Your mother is suffering," the doctors explained to Rachel. "We're only delaying her death, we're not helping her live."

"You're not listening to me!" Rachel exploded in response. "This meeting is loaded. You're not willing to explain to me what's going on or how we got here."

Bowman had been out of town and by the time he returned the ten-day-old battle was entrenched. The doctors had called the College of Physicians and Surgeons to ask if they had the right to discontinue treatment; the daughter had sought legal advice.

"Don't talk to me," Rachel finally said. "Talk to my lawyers."

She had no interest in speaking to Bowman either. He was, it seemed to her, just another hospital employee. But he asked if he could talk to her for a minute to hear her side. After letting her vent, he asked a few questions and all of a sudden they were in a conversation that lasted a couple of hours each day for three days. "If I hear the word *futile* one more time," she told him, "I'm going to scream." For days, it seemed, that word had punctuated every conversation she'd had in the hospital. People had repeatedly told her, "I want you to realize that you may want what's best for your mother, but this is futile."

Bowman, who is careful never to use that f-word, was the first person willing to listen to Rachel. And what he heard made him realize how the conflict had first flared up and how completely avoidable it had been—if only someone had taken the time to find out Dusana's story. Rachel's mother had grown up Catholic in Czechoslovakia, but in the late 1930s she had married a Jewish man and converted. Sixteen months later, when the Third Reich invaded, the Nazis arrested her at work and sent her to Auschwitz. There, they put her in one of the "research" areas and performed experiments on her. This experience gave her an enduring fear of death and medical procedures. Afterwards, she was reunited with her husband, who had escaped to London, and the couple moved to Canada and became devout Orthodox Jews.

Knowing how sacred life is in Judaism—in fact, he'd heard rabbis say, "A minute of life is equal to an eternity"—Bowman also realized that Rachel had picked up from Dusana an instinct for life that was non-negotiable, as well as an enormous and understandable fear of doctors and their authority. "What was under the tip of the iceberg was so huge, but it's not what medical teams look at or for," he said. "No one knew this woman was a Holocaust survivor. Nobody asked, and the daughter wasn't giving anything away because they'd pissed her off."

Although he finally got Rachel to talk to him, he didn't have a hope of putting her and the medical team together in the same room. So he had to use shuttle diplomacy. His goal was to get the doctors and nurses to stop talking about Dusana as a patient when they spoke to Rachel and to simply start referring to her as a person. Most doctors and nurses say they do that, and they probably even think they do, but Bowman is not convinced. While great ethical tension can be inevitable in end-of-life decisions, sometimes the problem is simply a failure to communicate. And miscommunication leads to conflict. If the medical team had connected earlier with a different side of Rachel, the dispute might never have reached the crisis point.

In the end, Bowman spent a week negotiating with the team on behalf of Rachel, who agreed to let the doctors try antibiotic therapy for a while, and if that didn't work she would accept their recommendation. Dusana died two weeks later.

FOR BOWMAN, it was a reminder that ethics is not always about highfalutin ideas: "I'd love to say these are great philosophical questions bumping up against each other, and to some extent they are, but part of this is ethics, and part is just humanity."

Sue MacRae calls it the Michelangelo principle. Solving an ethical problem requires carving away what doesn't belong to reveal what needs to happen. The right choice can emerge from a clash of values—one person's idea of quality of life is different from another's—if the two sides are open and honest with each other. "Suddenly, the sculpture is in front of you and you don't know how it got there."

Like most nurses, MacRae grappled with end-of-life dilemmas early on in her career. "From the first day you step into a hospital, a nurse faces death and dying on a number of levels, on a physical level of what it means for someone's body to die, but also at much deeper levels," she told me. "You're a person off the street when you start your nursing program and all of a sudden you're in the privileged position to watch the most unbelievable stuff related to human beings, the most profound being death."

That's what got her passionate about ethics. She found that she and her nursing colleagues were usually too busy dealing with the physical needs of their patients and had little time to go deeper into the difficult questions that abound on emotional, psychological and spiritual levels. Nurses, it seemed to her, were the ones who had the most exposure to death, and were involved in it from the closest vantage point, but they didn't often have the time to attend medical rounds to listen to ethical discussions. "Whether you're a religious person or an agnostic, you're still pushed to a place of questioning," she said. Nurses, especially those working in an emergency room or an ICU, have an intuition about these issues and will have to face them every day, because they're at the bedside with the patient. But too often hospitals don't provide the time or the place for ethical discussions to take place. "So the irony is they're the ones who are least prepared."

MacRae grew up in Calgary and graduated from nursing school in 1991. She went on to become the bioethicist at UNH, preceding Linda Wright, and later the deputy director of the JCB. She'd stopped seeing patients, but she did work with the clinical ethicists that are part of the centre. When I visited the red-haired McCrae in her small office there (she's since left the JCB), she wore a red dress, red leggings and sandals. She also sported a tiny stud in her right nostril. Smart, engaged and thoughtful, she was an animated speaker and wasn't afraid to laugh.

A doctor may face a particular ethical issue only once in his or her career while a clinical ethicist sees it many times. But even when ethicists think they've seen everything, along comes something even more unbelievable or profoundly difficult. So one of the advantages of putting a group of them together in a place like the JCB is that they get together every week to talk about the cases they're facing and share knowledge and experience. If a case came up at Mount Sinai that Bowman had never encountered, another ethicist could say, "Oh, we had something like that last year."

While that wealth of experience is invaluable, so is the variety of professions at the JCB, including doctors, social workers and lawyers. "I wouldn't want it any other way, because everyone has blind spots and everyone makes a contribution," said MacRae, who admitted that when she found herself being too practical— "being too much of a nurse"—she could ask a colleague to help her see the problem more philosophically.

Bioethics, she hopes, is an opportunity to hold a discussion across different worldviews. "The currency in health care is still technology and science and knowledge, and the experiential, feeling, intuition, soul of health care hasn't been given the same status," she said. "We're moving in that direction—where we bring science and soul together. We have to get there, because you can't have one without the other and we see the train wrecks when you try to have just a biotechnical model without a human, compassionate response to balance it." For now, doctors are still in charge of that knowledge, but MacRae suggested that the power may be shifting and that ten or fifteen years from now the scientists will have the power and the doctors will be the deliverers of the treatment. At that point, doctors may gain a better understanding of the way nurses feel today. (This thought made me wonder what to make of the fact that women now outnumber men in med schools while the education system struggles to get more women to enter science programs.)

For several years, those involved in clinical ethics have been asking, "What are we doing? What are we really offering to make a difference?" Every bioethicist has an answer, and many have written books and manuals and engaged in long discussions about "competencies" and standards, but few have thought to ask what the patients, the families, the doctors, the nurses and the senior administrators who were funding the programs thought. If hospital CEOs decide they want to build ethics into the system from boardroom to bedside, it can make a difference, but not if they just plunk someone in an office to look good when accreditation comes around. Seeing organizational ethics as being just as important as bedside issues represents a big shift in thinking. Bowman, who has increasingly devoted time to this at Mount Sinai, admitted, "The big question about ethicists is are we watchdogs or are we lapdogs? When a hospital appoints us, do they want us to make sure there's ethical practice or do they just want to put us on show so they can justify what they're doing?"

The answer, not surprisingly, depends on the hospital. Peg Tittle is a trained philosopher, author of books on ethics and now a self-described "ex-ethicist" who lives in Sundridge, Ontario, about an hour away from North Bay. In 1997, when she was teaching ethics at Nipissing University, she called up the North Bay General Hospital and offered to help. What she didn't realize was that the hospital's ethics committee—which was actually called the Ethics/Pastoral Care Committee—didn't have any professional ethicist on it at all. So she filled one of the two spots on the committee reserved for community members. But she grew increasingly frustrated over the next four years and finally quit in 2001.

The one area where Tittle made a difference was in research ethics, where she took two existing questionnaires and tailored them to the hospital. But she made no headway in her efforts to increase the ethics education of the others on the committee. She found that, like most people, they thought that what they'd learned from their parents was enough to get them through life. "I just want to cringe when someone says there's no expertise involved and we know right from wrong," she said. "Sorry, but once you're past about six years old, the ethical decisions you have to make are just not that simple." Tittle also failed to win any support for an ethics consultation process. In four years, no one at the hospital ever called on her to help with a case, preferring to go to the social worker or the chaplain. In a way, she really couldn't blame them. "Truth be told," she said, "if the ethics committee was just this group of people who met once a month and shuffled paper around, why would anyone bring anything to us?"

Today, more and more hospitals take ethics seriously and Sue MacRae is optimistic about the future of the field, though she would like to see bioethics find a common vision for itself. The goal should be to improve the quality of health care for everyone involved: patients, families and those providing the care. "Without that, it's meaningless to me," she insisted, though she admitted that other ethicists see it differently and prefer to play more of an activist role. "Ethics is fairly new, and I think it's going in the right direction unless it becomes too focused on its own autonomous role and its own entity. The danger is it becomes its own machine, its own silo, its own problem."

Doctors see more conflict these days, not less, which Mehta attributes to patients' and families' heightened expectations: "It's because patients are more educated, it's because of the existence of the internet and it's because the entitlement of the general population is increasing and anger toward the profession is increasing because of the long delays." While an oncologist or a surgeon can refuse to treat a patient if there's really no hope of making a difference, it's harder for an ICU doctor to refuse to do so, especially if families are vocal enough, litigious enough and adamant enough. Mehta worked in Quebec and Rhode Island before joining Mount Sinai, and found that U.S. patients tend to be even more demanding than Canadian ones—and hospitals, fearing litigation, usually give in. "It's not necessarily the best thing for the patient, but we will do it because it's the best thing for the family and it's the best thing for us personally to avoid further conflict. That's not the way we should practise medicine but that's often the way it is in the ICU."

With a diverse patient population holding potentially wildly different views on end-of-life care, and with everyone more willing to challenge the system, conflict is inevitable in hospitals. But Leslie Vincent, senior vice-president of nursing at Mount Sinai, argues that staff are better at dealing with it and there's been an improvement in the nature of the discussions and commitment to the process of consent. "What Kerry Bowman talks to me about is that he sees a greater depth of understanding and a greater appreciation for end-of-life issues," she told me, "so it's not so much about who makes the decision."

Indeed, Bowman has seen a significant decline of such conflict at Sinai over the last five years. If Mehta is right and she sees more, not less, that suggests doctors and nurses are doing a better job of dealing with it on their own. "I like to imagine—but I could be completely and utterly wrong—that it has to do with more progressive policies and a greater focus on conflict resolution rather than who's right and who's wrong," Bowman said. "I like to imagine that there's been enough of a culture shift at Sinai that we tend not to lock horns, that we tend to look at these things and say, 'Wow. That's ethically challenging,' rather than 'She's in denial.' It can't be that simple, but I hope there's some trend in that direction."

That's one reason he believes more strongly in his profession now than he did when he was getting his doctorate. "I can say from the bottom of my heart that I have more faith in the practice of clinical bioethics than I did when I started. I didn't not have faith, but I wasn't sure. I thought it could work, but now I know it can—not all the time and not in all cases—but I feel much more optimistic about it."

4 Faith and the Human Spirit
A mother's choice to continue treatment for her adult daughter

STEPHANIE HAD BEEN COMPLAINING about headaches for three or four years. "Don't worry," her doctor told her. "It's just stress or migraines." After all, such symptoms aren't uncommon among young women in their early thirties. But on the Canada Day long weekend in 1996, Stephanie's pain was greater than ever. Her mother, Janet, who was visiting from Jamaica, thought it was something to do with her eyes.

"Oh, Mom, you're always predicting."

"Well, you never know," Janet said, "one day I'm going to predict something right."

After the long weekend, Stephanie went to see her doctor again. He still thought she was suffering from migraines but sent her to an ophthalmologist. After dilating her eyes, the eye doctor could see something that concerned him and told her she needed a CAT scan as soon as possible.

At Toronto Western Hospital, neurosurgeon Mark Bernstein found a brain tumour and told Stephanie she had two options: he could operate on it or he could try to drain it. She wanted to get her ordeal over with, so she asked Bernstein to operate. On July 11, he removed a massive, spidery tumour that had worked its way into the tissue and veins of Stephanie's brain. And, as is often the case with such tumours, it bled and bled.

Before she could even speak to Stephanie, Janet saw orderlies wheeling her daughter from the recovery room back into the operating room. Stephanie was comatose and the prognosis was not good.

Janet was in Canada on a visitor's visa that would soon expire and she suddenly also had to worry about Stephanie's kids, a thirteen-year-old girl and an eleven-year-old boy. The nurses told her about Kerry Bowman and suggested she might want to speak to him. But Janet and Bowman kept leaving messages for each other at the nurse's station and it was a few days before they connected.

Although he had been a hospital social worker since 1986, Bowman was in the process of making the move into clinical ethics. In fact, he was just finishing his Ph.D. in bioethics. And Stephanie's case threatened to be difficult. She was in intensive care, extremely susceptible to infections and on a ventilator, but she was getting to the point where she would be breathing on her own. Once that happened, it meant surviving on a feeding tube and just drifting in a coma until ultimately succumbing to an infection. Bowman knew about Stephanie's case from rounds with the medical team and had heard how badly the operation had gone. He and Janet finally arranged to meet one afternoon at 2 p.m. He got to the ward an hour early to go over the chart and talk to the nurse. "It's not good to go in blind," he explained when he told me the story, "because you don't know fact from fiction."

And the facts in this case were not pretty. The CAT scans showed terrible damage and there was no potential for brain recovery. "Stephanie was not getting better at all," said Bowman. "We were coming to a decision about letting nature take its course. And let's be clear what that means: it means pulling the plug." Most people in comas need to be on life support machines, so withdrawing treatment can mean gradually reducing the support; or the family makes the decision that if the patient develops pneumonia—and people in these situations do develop pneumonia because their lungs are messy—the medical team should not do anything but control the pain.

Many families, facing the prospect of watching a loved one linger indefinitely, would opt to pull the plug. But since Bowman specializes in cultural differences in end-of-life issues, he was careful to find out exactly what Janet wanted. They met in a conference room. With their corporate feel—this one had about fifteen chairs around a large table and seemed better suited to a board meeting—such rooms don't provide the most intimate of settings, and Bowman, who has done hundreds of end-of-life consultations in his career, certainly never wants to end up sitting with family members "like Victorians at dinner time." He thinks about how he wants to sit and how he wants to hear what's being said—and what's not being said. "I lay it out for them, but I also try to draw out what the values of the person are and what their conflicts are and what their fears are about what they're going to live with in the future. I really try to blend the ethics with the context of the situation."

His social worker roots don't just come in handy in his job; that training shapes his whole approach. He wants to be as disarming as possible, because he doesn't want families to think he's going to psychologically dissect them or confront them. Besides, he believes that when people feel safe enough, they will tell him what they want him to know, so he wants to communicate—not just verbally—that he's open to talking about anything.

These meetings invariably take place at the worst possible time. The family members have just heard terrible news and are emotional and struggling to come to grips with the information.

But waiting would be worse, because there's usually a window of about twenty-four to forty-eight hours before the patient starts to breathe on his or her own and it's much easier to sort out an end-of-life decision when the patient is on a ventilator. Once the patient is breathing unassisted, the option of "pulling the plug" becomes even more traumatic because it means removing the feeding tube and watching the person slowly starve. Doctors are acutely aware of that and often send the message, "Do you realize she'll be breathing on her own by tomorrow?"

Bowman usually starts these meetings by explaining that he's someone who comes in when these difficult situations surface. "You can tell me anything you want," he'll say. "This is completely confidential. I'm not taking a position on this." Almost always, he's found, people start talking right away.

"PEOPLE CAN HAVE the Model T in any colour," carmaker Henry Ford is supposed to have said, "so long as it's black." Apocryphal or not, the line reflects the fact that Ford preferred black paint because it dried faster than any other colour. Since he couldn't keep up with demand for the Model T, a hugely popular car that stayed in production from 1908 to 1927, it just made sense to stick to black.

The danger for an ethicist doing an end-of-life consultation is the possibility of sounding too much like Henry Ford: "You must decide, but the choice needs to be what I think is best." Doctors and ethicists talk about autonomy as a central value, but Bowman admits that their commitment to it isn't always as strong as it should be. "When the family says we've thought about this and we don't think it's a meaningful life, we're so supportive. But when they say the opposite, that's when autonomy is suddenly, well..." His voice trailed off. "If we're going to say we believe in autonomy and choice, because it's the foundation of the health care system, then we can't complain when we get the wrong answer."

Back in July 1996, Bowman and Janet sat down close together in the conference room of the neuro-intensive care unit. Janet was very clear about not wanting to discontinue treatment—for personal and religious reasons. "Stephanie was alive so there was still hope," Bowman remembered. "I don't think she ever felt, in her heart of hearts, 'I just know my daughter is going to wake up.' It was nothing like that. I think it was about the respect for her life and that there's always the potential. I don't think she ever had any profound delusions." In a lot of his cases, Bowman and the family hash out all the painful ethics of the situation, but he and Janet didn't really go through any deep end-of-life decision making. "It really wasn't where she was at, and I felt it would have been inappropriate for me to raise it, because she was so clear," he said. "We could have talked for months, but she was so clear." Sometimes he senses ambivalence—that what people are saying initially is not what they'll say later. When a family is just not ready to let go, he will show some patience until they are ready. But with Janet, he sensed it was something deeper. It was just the way she saw it.

Only about one in ten families sees it that way. But Bowman was happy to respect Janet's wishes. While he didn't expect Stephanie to wake up, he had seen enough people in ICUs to know that doctors' predictions didn't always come to pass. He went to speak to Bernstein and braced himself for "a hell of a battle." Although the two would later write an ethics paper together, at the time they barely knew each other. But Bowman did know the culture of neurosurgery was macho and hierarchical—almost military—and not exactly open to suggestions from soft-hearted social worker types. Bernstein, however, had already spent time with Janet and developed a good rapport with her. He didn't have a problem with her decision.

Often, when there is a battle over a patient, especially one in Stephanie's condition, it has to do with resources. When someone with little or no chance for recovery takes a bed in the intensive care unit, there can be a great deal of pressure to make the most "practical" decision. That's the dirty little secret of health care in Canada: beds, equipment and staff are so scarce that hospitals sometimes make medical and ethical decisions based on those shortages. And while both Bowman and Bernstein respected Janet's choice, others didn't. "There were people on the periphery who thought this was a terrible waste of resources," said Bowman, who noted that some of his colleagues thought he should "encourage" her to make a different decision. "'Push' is the real word," he admitted after surprisingly little prodding. But he is not susceptible to peer pressure. What's right depends on the situation and the values of the people making the decision, so Bowman's main concern is "What would the patient have wanted?" Janet's best under-standing of what Stephanie would have wanted was life. He had never met Stephanie, had never had a conversation with her. He only knew her in a coma. "It's awful when you're at someone's bedside and always around and never have a conversation, but you absorb elements of who she is from her mother and her children. I would have been fine either way—I would have advocated either way—unless Janet was really torn. And many, many families are and they turn to an ethicist to say, 'I'm torn. What do you think? Let's work on this.'"

Once Stephanie was breathing on her own, she quickly trans-ferred out of the ICU and into a ward. That made the strain on the hospital's resources less acute. For her part, Janet didn't feel pressure from people in the hospital to make a different decision. "Maybe it was there," she admitted when I met her for a coffee in a busy mall in suburban Toronto, "but because I was concentrating on Stephanie, I wasn't concentrating on what they were saying."

Bowman, however, knew that some of his colleagues still thought Janet was in denial; some even said so. The thinking is: "They're in denial and the task for the health care workers— ethicists included—is to push them through it." But that's not how Bowman saw this case; in fact, he thought Stephanie's mother was fully aware of exactly what the situation was. "Janet just needed hope. I don't see hope and denial as the same thing. They're really not. But they get labelled that way."

AS STEPHANIE LAY in a coma, Janet stayed in her daughter's Scarborough apartment with her grandchildren and trekked downtown to the hospital every day. There, she bathed Stephanie and tended to her skin, her hair and her nails. She sang to her, read articles to her and talked to her. "It was actually a really beautiful thing to see," remembered Bowman. One day, Janet was at the hospital, standing at Stephanie's bedside crying. She felt someone touch her, and when she looked around it was Bowman. "You don't have to come every day," he told her. "Any day you don't feel like coming, call me and I will visit Stephanie and call you and tell you what's going on."

His kindness was a great relief for Janet, but it came as no great surprise. When she first met Bowman, she immediately felt comfortable with him. "There was some chemistry there, like we had known each other since long ago," she said. "Whatever I didn't understand, I could always call him and he would explain in layman's terms what the nurses were saying."

But her daughter's health, and the medical jargon, weren't Janet's only problems. She was also worried about the psychological health of her grandchildren, who were devastated. When Bernstein wanted to speak to them to explain their mother's situation, Bowman briefed them first. Later, he arranged for the kids to see a colleague who was a child psychologist. After seeing the shrink once, though, they refused to go again. Still, Bowman's colleague continued to offer advice that Bowman could pass on to Janet.

The other problem was Janet's legal status in Canada. Bowman put her in touch with an immigration lawyer and wrote letters on her behalf. He told immigration officials, "We're going to have a much bigger problem if you don't give this woman some help, because in about three weeks the Children's Aid Society is going to have two kids with emotional problems because their mother's in a coma and there's no one to take care of them."

While Janet sorted out her immigration problems, tended to her grandchildren and found supportive friends at church, her daughter remained a sleeping beauty. Stephanie was a lovely young woman with gorgeous skin and she looked like she could just wake up and walk out of the hospital at any moment— except that she needed a feeding tube to stay alive.

AS TIME PASSED, Bowman began to wonder if Stephanie might survive indefinitely. Sometimes a long-term patient going nowhere can be an irritant on a ward, leading to muted tensions and animosities. But that didn't happen here. Janet, a warm person who thinks the best of people and tends to get treated the same way in return, remained quite upbeat and never complained. That helped her befriend everyone on the ward. Only one nurse ever gave her attitude, and that happened only once. "Let's be honest, with Stephanie's case, one of the things that went right—well, Mark Bernstein was very good and fair about the whole thing—but if Stephanie had been on life support, I suspect that there would have been a lot more pressure," said Bowman. Some people might have pressured Janet to ask that doctors remove the feeding tube, but nobody did. The absence of conflict was unusual for a case like that. "Partly it was Janet and her personality, but it was partly also Mark and partly also me. We weren't that conflicted. Mark and I both saw that case in terms of 'She wants treatment. Fine.' There was no problem with that. It was her daughter. And that was it. And I'm not trying to blow our horns, but there are people who would not have accepted that."

Still, the hospital eventually considered moving Stephanie to Providence Villa, a long-term care facility in the east end of the city. But in July 1998, two years and a day after she'd gone into a coma, she died. (Two weeks later, the papers confirming her mother's landed immigrant status arrived in the mail. Janet, who'd been a factory supervisor in Jamaica but had always wanted to be a nurse, went to school to become a personal support worker and, coincidentally, ended up working at Providence Villa from 1999 until she retired in 2003.)

Bowman, who still meets with Janet for coffee, remains convinced that Stephanie did not suffer and was comfortable when she died. For him, the experience was a remarkable display of the human spirit. "Janet really rose to a very difficult situation," he said. "She found the fortitude from within to raise those kids to the best of her ability, to come to a foreign country, to get through the immigration process, to get status, to get a job. Watching Janet care for her daughter really stays with me, and I've watched lots of people spending time with people in comas."

Janet devoted a good deal of that time, with and without friends, to praying at her daughter's bedside. An Anglican, she found that her faith was, as ever, a source of tremendous strength and support. And though she and Bowman never really got into the ethics of the end-of-life decision she had to make, she knows she made the right choice. When Stephanie died, Janet was ready. "From day one, Dr. Bernstein had told me that she could go at any time," she remembered. "From day one it went into day two and then day three and then two years, so it gave me a long time to get myself well prepared. And of course I also asked the Lord to put me in a place where, anything comes, I can take it."

5 Mindfulness
The making of an ethicist

MOST OF THE STREETS in Bukavu were shattered. Little roadwork had been done in the city in eastern Democratic Republic of Congo since the Belgians left in 1960. So, even in 2004, Kerry Bowman and three conservation colleagues had to drive slowly on the way back to their hotel. They'd gone out for dinner because the hotel restaurant was expensive and, as always, money was tight. Suddenly, they came upon a roadblock on a dark stretch of the hilly road. They were within the city limits, but in an isolated area surrounded by trees and bushes, and although military roadblocks were common, the soldiers usually set them up at intersections or on busy routes and marked them with flags or lanterns. This one appeared much more informal.

The men at the roadblock carried submachine guns, and one of them ordered everyone out of the Jeep. The others—two Congolese and an American—climbed out, but Bowman stayed in the back seat. "It didn't feel right," he told me a few months later. "I just sat there and waited. Buddhists say that the first thing to do in a difficult situation is do nothing. I didn't have a plan at all, but I just thought I would do nothing for a second."

When the man repeated the order, Bowman said, "Oh, I'm sorry I don't understand French." Then, sensing a moment when everyone was distracted, he jumped out of the Jeep on the forest side, slammed the door, dropped to the ground and scrambled into the trees. Bowman was carrying $7,500 US in cash to pay locals who helped protect the apes from poachers and to fund small-scale initiatives designed to wean the community off hunting endangered species. He did not want to lose this money.

Bowman's ape activism regularly takes him to Africa, and while it may seem like a bizarre distraction for a clinical ethicist with a heavy caseload, he believes the two pursuits are connected. And the more I talked to him about it, the more I realized he was right and that his attitude toward his conservation work illuminated his approach to his job at Mount Sinai.

He started working with apes by chance. After graduating in 1979 with a degree in clinical psychology from Toronto's York University, he spent four and a half years backpacking around the world. While in a bar, he met some people who worked with orangutans and were looking for help, so he started following apes through the forests of Sumatra to identify their eating habits and nesting behaviour.

He was hooked. Years later, in 1994, he worked as a research assistant at Camp Leakey in Borneo and then became a research associate with The Gorilla/Chimpanzee Protection Project in the Republic of Cameroon and the Republic of Congo, working on the development of gorilla and chimpanzee conservation programs. In 2000, *University of Toronto Magazine* named Bowman—who did a master's of social work and a Ph.D. in bioethics there—to its list of "100 Alumni Who Shaped the Century." That same year, he launched his own conservation organization dedicated to preserving primates. Originally called the Great Ape Alliance, it's now known as the Canadian Ape Alliance. He's also been on the board of the Jane Goodall Institute since 2003.

Even without nighttime stickups, the work is dangerous, and some doctors back home challenge him about the risks, which they see as unjustifiable. "Of course," he noted, "they've never been there." And since the outlook for the great apes in the region where Bowman works is not promising, the same "very accomplished physicians" claim his conservation work is not a good use of his time. But not being a man of science, he sees things differently: "I'm not a believer in, if the job's difficult, you don't do it, or you don't try to do your best to do it."

To control the risks, Bowman developed strong relationships with both the government and local warlords who held power in large parts of the country in a devastating civil war that started in 1998 and officially ended with an uneasy peace late in 2003. Even today, the violence continues in the Kivu region, so he knows that such bonds take on greater meaning in the Congo: "If you damage a relationship, you could lose your life." But as he scurried into the forest that night of the ambush, he knew no amount of sweet-talking would help him out of this jam. After hiding the money under a log, he lay flat on the ground with no intention of coming out of the thick cover. He had things crawling all over him, but that was the least of his worries.

We'd met in a crowded restaurant on Toronto's Queen Street—a universe away from the Congo—to catch up, and when I'd arrived he was drinking a glass of white wine and reading a travel guide to Brazil in preparation for another, less adventurous, trip. A thick-bodied man with bushy eyebrows and a calm but focused energy, he never seems completely relaxed. Friendly and patient, he's not condescending, even when faced with my stupider questions, but neither is he likely to linger. He always has somewhere else to go, something that must be done.

Despite the critters in the Congolese bush, he was more concerned about his colleagues, because the robbers had grabbed their wallets and Bowman could hear a lot of angry yelling. He wanted to stay where he was, but he could see by the Jeep's headlights that the robbers were getting very aggressive and his Congolese friends were resisting. In an attempt to create a diversion, rather than as an act of bravery, he emerged from the forest.

He'd left the money in the woods, but kept his wallet, knowing that if he'd had nothing on him, the robbers would just drag him back into the forest. As he emerged from the bush, a robber grabbed him by the throat and jammed a submachine gun into his chest. Bowman, who'd only moments before claimed he couldn't speak French, told him, "*Monsieur, restez tranquil, s'il vous plaît.*" The gunman grabbed his wallet and pulled out a credit card. Although not many places in the Congo take plastic, and it would have been easy to call VISA anyway, Bowman said, "If you take that card, they can trace you and you'll get caught." Just as the gunman handed it back, lights appeared on the road and the bandits took off.

While his colleagues had lost everything—money, passports, wallets—Bowman had lost nothing except a button on his shirt. When they got back to the hotel, his knees went weak. He ordered a Scotch, and when the bartender offered him a small one, Bowman told him to keep pouring. "It sounds like I was very clever, but I wasn't," he recalled. "I was just taking it second by second. I had no plan; it just unfurled."

As terrifying as the experience was, it could have been a lot worse: on the next two nights, people travelling that same road ended up dead. Bowman, who never struck me as someone who tries to project a macho image and is not given to braggadocio, told me, "I'm less cautious now than when I was twenty. It's terrible! I'm doing all the wrong things for middle age."

This middle-aged social-worker-turned-ethicist may, initially, seem like the last person to risk his life for a few thousand bucks. But his gentle demeanour belies the passion, the commitment and the mental discipline that have helped him succeed in his parallel careers: bioethicist and conservationist.

ORIGINALLY FROM MONTREAL, Bowman has also lived in Hong Kong, Australia and Africa. In the late eighties, he spent a year travelling through that continent and worked in a British Oxfam refugee camp in Sudan and a Canadian Red Cross refugee camp in Ethiopia, where they buried children who had died of totally treatable afflictions. After completing a degree in social work at the University of British Columbia, Bowman returned to Toronto Western Hospital, located near the city's original Chinatown, where he had worked before his travels. This time, he took a job as a social worker in the intensive care unit.

He was struck by the diversity of the patients, but also by some of the insensitivity to that diversity. The ICU, for example, which faced west, overlooked a funeral home, and one of the rooms had two fours in its number even though four represents death in Chinese culture. "Setting sun, funeral home, fours all over the door," Bowman said, clapping his hands for emphasis before adding with a rueful laugh: "Like, come here to snuff it. All the omens were, 'You're never going to get out of this room, you're just going to die here.'"

Worse, his colleagues expected end-of-life decisions to be made based on the concept of autonomy, which is a basic premise in the *Canada Health Act*. The way that translates into an end-of-life decision is captured by questions such as: "If your father could speak for himself, what would he want us to do?" After living and working overseas, Bowman knew that question wasn't always the right one. "To a traditional Chinese family," he explained, "that question is from Mars."

Most of us assume autonomy is a universal concept, and it feels so right to us that we never question it, but in some cultures the moral framework is not about autonomy and independence, it's about interdependence, and morality is defined through webs of relationships. "A family's duty is to a sick loved one, and it's not about what this person would say," Bowman said. "It's a collective, shared decision." Faced with this confusion, many family members stayed silent or talked about what they thought was best, which left the health care workers thinking they were ignoring the question or unwilling to even look at what their loved one would want. To the medical team, it was selfishness. But Bowman recognized it as a cultural difference and decided to go back to school to study it. In 1992, he started a Ph.D. in bioethics at the University of Toronto and finished it in 1996. His doctoral thesis was on Chinese-Canadian attitudes toward end-of-life decisions. He also did a fellowship in cultural psychiatry. All the while, he kept working at Toronto Western.

In 1999, he became the clinical bioethicist at Mount Sinai, located on "Hospital Row." Close to half of its patients are from non-Western cultures and so are many of the doctors and nurses, but it's naive to assume, as I did, that a diverse staff solves all the cultural problems. "I've gotten in trouble for saying this, but I still believe it's true: many of the people from the developing world who come into medicine—not all, but many—are from a very high socioeconomic bracket and most of these countries have no middle class as we know it. Many, but not all, patients coming in are from much lower socioeconomic status, including refugee status, including coming with nothing." And just because two people come from the same country doesn't mean they share an ethnic background either; Cameroon, for example, is home to over two hundred ethnicities.

The more common problems, though, occur when people from other cultures must contend with Western values and notions. Brain death, for example, is complicated at the best of times, but throw in cultural differences and it gets worse. In Canada, if a patient is brain dead, he or she is legally dead, and doctors should pull the plug within twenty-four hours rather than continue to ventilate a dead person. It's not just that this is the accepted practice: it makes organ donations possible. But for many people from other parts of the world, it is as controversial as abortion. They don't understand brain death and don't accept it as a definitive diagnosis. Bowman, who has written papers on this subject, has had to look into the faces of family members who had no idea there was such a concept, let alone appreciate its legal significance. And yet the doctors have told them that their son—a twenty-year-old trauma victim, for example, who has rosy cheeks and whose chest rises and falls—is dead. In one case, the family started to make the appropriate arrangements, but upon hearing the deceased was in a bed and on a ventilator, the funeral home said, "Phone back when he's dead." So the family told the medical team, "The funeral home doesn't think he's dead."

Bowman admits such situations would be comical if they weren't so painful. "It's like a Monty Python skit," he said. "But it's a nightmare for families." His approach in a case like this is to talk to family members about what they think death is. He says as little as possible and lets them talk.

While culture—or at least our misunderstanding of cultural differences—can pose problems, religion usually helps more than it hinders. True, the attitude toward life in some religions can be a source of conflict, but faith helps believers come to terms with death. "Religion in end-of-life is often a blessing, to use a corny term, because it gives people strength and solace,"

Bowman said. "Religion is willing to face death—and the questions associated with death. Nothing else is."

AS BOWMAN STUDIED ethics in the 1990s, he became increasingly fascinated by ethical questions concerning the great apes. We share as much as 98.7 percent of our DNA with apes, who are, in fact, closer to humans than to monkeys (one of his pet peeves is people who confuse monkeys and apes). While there's a lot that separates us in the remaining DNA, we're genetic kin. And yet they're being pushed to extinction, largely due to the bushmeat trade in Africa and deforestation in the Far East.

Inevitably, some critics accuse him of worrying more about animals than humans, especially when so many people are dying in Africa, but Bowman doesn't see how anyone can separate the two issues. Others agree: Marie Adsett was a reporter for a television station in Hamilton, Ontario, when her assignment editor passed her a fax promoting a speech about apes at the Toronto Zoo. Adsett ended up not covering the event, but she was intrigued enough to call up the speaker and say, "I need to meet you." And she was so impressed with Bowman that she became a volunteer (mostly doing communications work) for the Canadian Ape Alliance. In September 2005, she accompanied him to Africa on a ten-day trip. At a sanctuary, she saw how well he interacted with apes. "It's something special and magical," she said. "He understands them and they feel it. You should see them take to him."

But Adsett found Bowman's connection to the people even more inspiring. And she noted the calm presence and creative mind that's helped him in the ICU and in the Congo. "He can quickly turn things around," she said. "He takes it all in and starts thinking and processing it." She also saw his compassion, and how heart-breaking the work can be, when they visited a genocide museum, met with the widows of park rangers who'd been trying to protect the apes, or got together with some women who had suffered miscarriages—an even more serious matter in that culture because being able to produce children is so crucial. As he left the meeting with the women, he said to Adsett, "This is what I deal with every day at work."

JUST AS BOWMAN'S JOB as an ethicist informs his work as a conservationist, his background as a social worker shapes his approach to performing as an ethicist. People from many different backgrounds, including medicine, law and administration, go into ethics, and these first careers help define what kind of ethicist they become. Bowman compares an ethicist's first profession to a first language, an intriguing metaphor given that ethicists with a social work background struck me from the start as better communicators and more at ease with people.

When I asked Bowman about this, he reluctantly admitted that he might have better communication skills than some, but quickly added that he lacks skills other ethicists have, including medical or legal knowledge. And sometimes the mindset of his first career can be restrictive. "Social work can be limiting," he said. "I liked being a social worker, but the profession itself, now that I look back, has some real blind spots. Social workers are not as creative or open as you might think; they can be very stuck in certain ways of thinking."

Another social-worker-turned-ethicist is Karen Faith, the director of the clinical ethics centre at Sunnybrook and Women's Hospital and someone who describes Bowman as a mentor. She admitted that while the two occupations sometimes appear to be similar, the focus and roles are quite different. But she believes Bowman's experience as an ICU social worker is an asset. "Kerry has a familiarity with difficult emotional and psychological issues that folks in a more academic setting wouldn't necessarily encounter on a regular basis," she said. "It's never comfortable for us to witness the pain of others, but I think you become familiar with it and learn how to witness that pain."

Michael Campbell, Bowman's former assistant, described his old boss's approach as more anthropological than philosophical. And according to Shawn Richard, who worked with Bowman at Mount Sinai, "The first thing Kerry thinks about are the relationships between people, whereas a lot of bioethicists first think about the theoretical issues. They have more of a top-down approach, and a lot of times the implications for the parties are secondary."

Philosophers sometimes just shrug when Bowman talks about his approach to conflict resolution. "They don't know where to go with it," he said, "because it has nothing to do with philosophy." That doesn't mean he'd like to see his profession taken over by social workers who've had some ethical training but have no real understanding of the philosophy, because that would just be glorified social work. "The thing about ethics is, it's not about advocacy in all cases," he said, adding that any ethicist who comes from a different discipline has to unlearn some of what he or she knows. "Ethics is about what ought to be done. That's not really the same principle as social work."

When it comes to doing what ought to be done, Bowman tends to be more practical than philosophical, though practical is far different from expedient. To illustrate his approach, Bowman gave me an example of a situation he's faced more than once: A young, healthy woman shows up in Emerg forty weeks pregnant and in labour. When the doctors realize vaginal delivery isn't possible, they recommend an emergency C-section, but she absolutely refuses on cultural grounds. She sees it as a violation of her integrity and femininity. "This is not done where

I'm from," insists the woman, who is from Somalia. And her husband fully supports her. That leaves the medical team with a patient saying she doesn't want a procedure and a baby that will die without that procedure. "It really tests the limits of pluralism in our society," said Bowman. "You have to respect this person's autonomy, and you also have an unborn child, which doesn't have any legal rights in Canada, but that doesn't mean on moral grounds people aren't going to feel the horror of that." For Bowman, it's a situation that calls for more direct action. While the woman may not want to hear the bad news from him or the doctors, she might listen to someone from her own community. So he quickly finds a community leader who will advise her to go ahead with the Caesarean. Sometimes that's worked; other times, it hasn't.

The philosophical grounding of the discipline makes it easy to frame everything as an either–or problem. So *either* doctors provide an emergency C-section *or* she dies. "Now, philosophically—and I say this in a very guarded way—that's an interesting point to make for ethical teaching," Bowman mused. But his job is to solve problems. "I have to be very careful about getting into either–or dilemmas. You have to be very creative and find some middle path that hasn't been thought of before."

An example he uses when teaching health care workers is the case of a ninety-one-year-old man who was born in Imperial China. Suffering from severe lung disease, he was on a ventilator, though he could sit up and read the newspaper. Several times over seven or eight weeks, his doctors had attempted to wean him from his ventilator but failed. His five kids, who were born in Hong Kong, begged doctors not to tell their father he could not be taken off the machine. His grandchildren, all born in Canada and mostly young professionals, told their parents to trust the doctors, but the second generation wanted more time, especially since they weren't completely convinced the Western approach was best and wanted to try acupuncture. They also insisted on staying positive, because in their culture it would be cruel and unfair to tell someone he was trapped on a machine: letting him know death was inevitable would be like a curse. (After Bowman tried to explain living wills to one elderly Chinese woman, she actually said, "Why are you putting this curse on me?")

The doctors, who wanted to withdraw treatment, believed they had to tell the truth, for legal reasons if nothing else. But in Chinese culture, one of the five foundations of Confucian thought is the strong duty of children to parents. So what should an ethicist do? Are there limits to autonomy in the face of such cultural differences? Was he obligated to tell the man?

Bowman's solution was to go to him and say, "We have medical information for you. Do you want us to tell you or do you want us to deal with your children?" This patient wanted to hear the news, but Bowman has said the same thing to patients in similar circumstances and they've responded the other way. After the doctors told the man the truth, as cautiously as possible, he asked to be left alone for two weeks. The doctors weren't happy about it, but Bowman backed the man. Two weeks later, they took him off the ventilator and he died.

ONE EARLY SPRING DAY I drove to Sudbury, four hours north of Toronto, to see Bowman speak at Science North about his ape work. In two days at the science centre, he gave three versions of the one talk. Although most of the material was the same, he skillfully tailored his delivery for each audience: an afternoon crowd dominated by schoolchildren, adults in the evening and high school students the next morning. The nighttime lecture attracted a large and appreciative crowd in a big room with jagged rock walls cut out of the Canadian Shield.

Though he's worked with all of the great apes, Bowman has a particular interest in bonobos, the least known of the four great ape species. Found only south of the Congo River, bonobos are endangered, with fewer than ten thousand left. Traditionally, some Congolese tribes protected them, considering them kin. "In their mythology, they and the bonobos lived together in a large village long ago, and when the people began to wear clothes, the bonobos didn't want to and they moved into the forest," Bowman explained to the audience. "It's not a long way from the truth." But food shortages, exacerbated by the civil war, led bushmeat hunters to start killing bonobos. Bushmeat, from animals that aren't considered traditional game, includes everything from rats to monkeys to elephants—as well as gorillas, chimpanzees and bonobos. The growth in the trade since the mid-1990s has alarmed conservationists, who thought they'd been making gains in the battle to save the great apes. The situation now appears increasingly grim.

Bowman's lecture included some gory slides that he didn't show the kids in his other talks (he warned the audience and apologized if it disturbed anyone, but said he wasn't prepared to sugar-coat what was going on). Despite the serious subject, he often amused the crowd. When he showed a map of the two countries named Congo—the Democratic Republic of Congo (formerly Zaire) and the Republic of Congo—he added, "You can tell them apart because it's the democratic one that doesn't allow elections."

He really got the audience going when he discussed the sex life of bonobos. Pointing out that a lot of assumptions about human nature are wrong because they're based on cultural values, he cited the belief that a patriarchal society is inevitable because the males dominate among higher primates. But bonobos are matriarchal. Similarly, people who see human violence as natural and unavoidable are ignoring the fact that bonobos, unlike the occasionally warlike chimpanzees, are not violent. "They mediate all social tension, hierarchy, conflict through sexual relations," Bowman explained. "So they have sex a lot." The crowd chuckled. "This is why the zoos are not always so thrilled with having a lot of them around, because of school tours and things." The audience laughed harder. "And they're very creative. I don't want to embarrass myself or you any further, but trust me on this," he continued over the roar, "it's phenomenal. You have no idea. And there's another assumption about human behaviour: that any form of sexuality outside of reproduction is sick, abnormal, not within the natural world." Despite the laughs he scored, I found it hard not to see his comments as a shot at religious conservatives. "You should see bonobos. It's not about reproduction, because they aren't doing it the right way for reproduction."

The humour aside, he alternated between sounding like an activist and sounding like an ethicist. Well-spoken, opinionated and willing to challenge his audience, he made no secret of his dislike for the European logging companies active in Africa, the bushmeat trade and the mining of a metallic ore called coltan, short for columbite-tantalite, which is used in cellphones, video game machines and other electronic devices. And he blamed the media for not covering the issues—a standard activist trope. Other times, though, he sounded more like an ethicist, weighing both sides carefully and then explaining his decision. He told the audience the story of buying an orphan chimpanzee. "It's a big ethical question, because one could argue that what you're doing is encouraging this," he admitted, noting that if he buys a chimpanzee for as little as five or ten dollars, the seller will just go out and get more chimps because he's just been shown there's a market for them. But doing nothing is a death sentence, because when people get bored with the chimp, or it bites somebody, they will eat it. "And this is not a good outcome either, as far as I'm concerned," he argued, adding that taking chimpanzees to a sanctuary where they can live with their own kind and eventually have a semi-release means that their life matters. "So I choose to buy it. It may be the wrong answer but knowing it would die, I personally could not leave it. I thought it was wrong."

Bowman's ability to see both sides is essential to his success as a clinical ethicist. "He sees the viewpoint of others and tries to find common ground or help them to see a different viewpoint and move them away if they're entrenched," said Leslie Vincent, who as senior vice-president of nursing at Mount Sinai is Bowman's boss. She also praised him for his ability to help hospital staff separate their values from patients' values, a particularly useful skill during conflicts over end-of-life decisions. "He's got to be a calm presence and a good listener as well as be willing to provoke a little bit." Most of all, the job requires strong communication skills, which is why Vincent appreciates Bowman's ability to translate the language of bioethics, to reframe issues from another perspective and to really listen. "He's listening to what you're saying; he's not thinking about the next thing he's going to say all the time," she said. "When he's with you, he's really with you."

IF THE CLASH of cultures were the only source of conflict in the modern hospital, a clinical bioethicist's job would be hard enough. But there are plenty of other issues to fight over. Disputes within families, for example, are common. Sometimes it's as simple as the Cousin from California syndrome: the son who moved away wants everything done to save his father, while the daughter who lives near their dying dad and has watched him deteriorate believes it would be better to just let him go. Often it has more to do with stress and inadequate sleep than anything else, so doctors and clinical ethicists will tell the family members to go home, get a good night's sleep and they can talk again the next day.

Sometimes, though, there's more to it. The daughter demanding extraordinary measures for her mother might actually be haunted by the fact that the last time she and her mother spoke they had a spat and she never apologized. And there's nothing like an end-of-life situation to re-ignite long-simmering family rivalries, animosities and hurt feelings. Respirologist and ICU doctor Sangeeta Mehta remembers the case of an elderly woman who was very ill and in intensive care. Her husband wanted everything done for her, which upset their children, who were estranged from the father. One even faxed a letter to him that read: "You asshole, you're making our mother suffer. I'll get you for this." Mehta was shocked. "There are very dysfunctional families out there," she told me. "It makes you appreciate your own family."

Patients' loved ones also fear that the doctors or the hospital will make decisions based more on financial concerns than what's best for the patient. Some people, when asked to agree to a Do Not Resuscitate order for a loved one, angrily respond, "You're just trying to save the government money." The bitterness can be even greater when it comes to ICU beds. Mehta, for example, has heard many families say, "Oh, you must need the bed," and suggest that the hospital doesn't want to keep a patient alive because it's a waste of resources. "That's never our thinking. Never," she insisted. She allowed that doctors do sometimes think about beds when moving patients to a ward, but not when it comes to withdrawing care. "We would never suggest withdrawing care from a patient because there are three other patients waiting for that bed. That's not what physicians do."

Maybe Mehta doesn't, but Bowman has certainly seen plenty of pressure to let a patient go. "Bed blocker" is not an uncommon term in hospitals, which are designed for acute patients, not those with chronic afflictions; the attitude is "Get 'em better and get 'em out, or let 'em die and get 'em out." Finances definitely do play a role, especially since dying can take a long time. "I do not believe that you can tell families that you see their loved one as a sinkhole," said Bowman, who admitted that in some cases that's what the family has thought they heard, and in others, because of poor communication skills, that's exactly what was said. "The fact that somebody's mother is eighty-six is not the point, and they do not want to be told that the medical team does not see her as a good use of money."

Still, he has sympathy for the doctors, especially since the health care system expects them to do more with less. "Resource allocation is absolutely an ethical question," he said. "But bringing resource allocation decisions or questions to the bedside is absolutely unethical." The people who run the hospital are the ones who need to make the decisions about how they want to run their ICU and determine how many people the unit will take and using what criteria.

Bowman's sympathy is not necessarily reciprocated. No matter how good an ethicist he is, he can't avoid running into that sense of superiority that some doctors brandish. Shawn Richard has seen doctors be downright hostile to Bowman and has watched how he's handled it. Sometimes Bowman has stood his ground—when it's concerned something worth fighting over, like informed consent, for example. Other times, he has deferred. But anyone who mistakes that as a lack of backbone is a fool, according to Richard. "The way he looks at is, there's no point in constantly being in people's faces," he told me. "There are a lot of things I learned from Kerry, but one of them was just watching your surroundings, choosing your battles and realizing when it's in your best interest to resist and when sometimes you just have to swallow it as part of the process of trying to get to some sort of resolution."

And even if some doctors can't hide their arrogance, others are fans. Mehta praises Bowman for being an excellent listener, a good judge of character and someone who is articulate and expressive—all traits that make for a strong bioethicist. He is also not judgmental and doesn't allow his personal beliefs to come through. Occasionally, though, she wishes he were more decisive. "He's someone who does see both sides of the story," she said, "but sometimes we'll find that Kerry sits on the fence."

Coming from a doctor, that may just be code for wanting him to back her up more, but Richard also admitted that Bowman's approach can flirt with paralysis by analysis. A case that still haunts him is one they worked on in 2001. It involved a dying woman who was in severe pain, and it seemed, to Richard anyway, that no one particularly cared. The medical team, who said the patient was difficult, declared the woman incompetent, so her brother was making all the health care decisions on her behalf, even though the siblings hadn't spoken in well over a decade and she specifically said she didn't want him to speak for her. After a week of talking to the woman, Richard was convinced that even though she was in pain and hadn't slept in a week, she was far more lucid than a lot of other people who are deemed competent. He wanted to stand up to the doctors and say, "Okay, you people have to do something now. You've got to deal with this situation." Bowman's tack, on the other hand, was to be more cautious, working slowly, trying to get more information and quietly changing people's opinions.

A week later, Bowman and Richard stood outside Mount Sinai on Toronto's University Avenue, arguing about the case.

Meanwhile, inside the hospital, the woman died. "She died in pain, and my feeling was we hadn't done enough. I didn't have a lot of experience clinically, but I felt the approach was just all wrong," said Richard. Though their disagreement did not affect their friendship or their working relationship, he added, "I was completely unsettled by it and it left us both with baggage."

WHILE AT SCIENCE NORTH, Bowman told the audience about how he treated sick children in Africa. "It was kind of a nightmare for me, because I'm scared of getting the dosages wrong," he admitted, "but I had to do something, and I eventually was running a clinic myself, which is a pretty terrible thing for an ethicist to do."

That line earned Bowman another big laugh, even if he didn't mean it to be funny. But it was an example of how his two disparate passions intersect more often than might at first seem likely. "He's a student of human behaviour," said Leslie Vincent, and it's not hard to draw a link to his former job as researcher studying orangutans years earlier.

Sometimes when he's in Africa he's able to take advantage of his connection to a hospital. In a Cameroon ape sanctuary, for example, he wanted to help a tiny three-week-old gorilla who had a bad chest infection and was close to dying. He got on the phone with the neonatal intensive care unit at Mount Sinai and explained that he had a six-pound baby and, using all the medical lingo, gave a full description of the symptoms. The staff told Bowman, who had a big drug kit with him, what to give the patient. The gorilla soon enjoyed a full recovery. "I didn't even mention that he wasn't actually human," Bowman admitted, "but they know me and I think they suspected."

The death of a gorilla in California also called for Bowman's unusual combination of skills. Michael, companion to Koko, the famous gorilla who understands a good deal of English and has a vocabulary of over a thousand signs, died in 2000 of a heart attack at the age of twenty-seven. Koko became withdrawn and showed all the classic signs of bereavement, including crying, decreased appetite and trouble sleeping. The Gorilla Foundation, just outside San Francisco, where the two gorillas lived, wanted someone who had experience with both apes and bereavement therapy. "I guess that's a pretty narrow list," laughed Bowman.

He flew down and began to work with the gorilla. "It wasn't a lot different than it is with a human child. Koko paints and Koko has toys, so play and art therapy were really the way to go," he explained. He also spent a lot of time doing one-to-one sessions with the devastated staff because he's found that a lot of people who work with apes develop extremely intense attachments to them—attachments beyond the ones humans form with other animals, perhaps because the apes are endangered. And it was as much a challenge working with the staff as it was with Koko. He spent a week or so there and hopes he helped. "It's hard to know with any bereavement work whether you've made a difference or not. I tried."

A few years ago, the Toronto Zoo approached him about becoming its ethics consultant, though nothing ever came of it. But it was one more reminder of how his life's goals are connected. Although he knows we may be within ten years of losing all of the great apes, he's not without hope. Mountain gorillas, a species he doesn't work with, are making a comeback because of conservation work. And the number of concerned people continues to grow. Even the warlords care because they're smart enough to understand the connection between the environment and survival of the people. "I think," said Bowman, "it can be done."

AS A CONSERVATIONIST, Bowman seeks to influence, but in his other job he's uncomfortable about doing that. Not all ethicists share his reluctance, though. In fact, for "public issue" ethicists, taking strong stands on difficult subjects is their job. They write op-ed pieces, make media appearances and take on speaking engagements. "The goal on the clinic side is to improve the experience of patients and their families," Peter Singer told me. "The goal on the public issue side is not to necessarily convince people of the rightness of my position; it's to make sure that people understand the issues at stake so it's an informed decision, and democratic deliberation is better. It's a very constructive vision of bioethics." As one of the country's most prominent ethicists and a regular contributor to the op-ed pages, Singer believes his role is to increase public awareness and understanding in order to improve the debate, not to win it.

I have my doubts that anyone in any profession could happily accept being on the losing side of an argument, but the attraction of having a podium is obvious. When I first met Bowman early in 2003, he made a clear distinction between what he did as a clinical ethicist and what public issue ethicists do. "There are many ethicists—often the high-profile ones—who take positions on things," he told me. "I don't have the profile or the inclination to do that. And clinicians—the front-line people—tend to do less of that, because we're already dealing with a patient, a family and a team. I think if you come out with, 'This is what should happen and this is what shouldn't happen,' you're unlikely to be asked back."

But over time, Bowman has increasingly become a go-to guy for the media, getting quoted on many issues, ranging from organ transplants to assisted suicide. In some ways this has been a natural progression for someone who, in order to promote his ape work, has had to learn how the media operate.

Promoting a conservation organization in the hope of generating both money and awareness is one thing, but speaking out on controversial ethical issues is quite another. Public issue ethicists working out of universities have academic tenure, so they can't get fired no matter what they say. The one thing these commentators have in common is they don't see patients. As a professor, Bowman has protection, but he also deals with patients and their families, so speaking out on controversial cases is something he worries about. "Part of it is the growth you go through as a person or an ethicist, where you realize you actually do have opinions," he told me. "It's very hard as a clinician to be taking positions." Initially, when the media called, he tried to keep his comments to outlining the case and explaining the ethical questions without taking a strong stand one way or another. But in May of 2005, there was the case of a fourteen-year-old Jehovah's Witness with cancer who didn't want a blood transfusion. A judge in British Columbia had ruled she could not refuse the treatment, because the court's authority to protect her life and safety was greater than her right to make her own choice on medical matters. So she fled to Toronto to get a second opinion, asking a court to let her go the States to receive treatment that didn't require a blood transfusion. But the Ontario judge sent her back to B.C. because he couldn't find any fault with the original ruling.

Bowman's take was that if she was a competent and mature minor, and there weren't factors he didn't know about—which was possible—the ruling was a violation of her right to make her own decision. "In this country, respect for religion is very high on the list. And this is about religion and people kept saying it's not about religion, it's about child welfare. But it is." And he didn't have much time for those who claimed the girl wasn't competent because she had said she wanted to live yet didn't want a transfusion. He didn't think "I don't want blood, but I want to live" was a confusing message at all. "If you want to be very cold, clinical, logical about it, from a medical point of view, you could argue it is," he said to me. "But if you look at it in a broader context of religious belief systems, I think it's actually the workings of a pretty limited perspective to say that's inconsistent. The transfusion is a violation of her views of the universe and religious law." Some people told him privately that the case was a no-brainer and that he shouldn't criticize a judge for sending her back, because she was on the run and was a ward of the state and the law was clear. But law and ethics are not the same. "I'm not a lawyer and I wasn't asked to comment on the law," Bowman said. "I'm talking about what ought to be done, and I see a huge conflict on religious grounds. To force blood on someone—if she believes she's going to burn in hell for eternity it is not a good outcome."

That Bowman spoke out so emphatically on this case is an indication of how strongly he feels about autonomy. And it bothered him that the case of Terry Schiavo had sparked such front-page hype while coverage of the Jehovah's Witness teenager later that same year was buried well inside newspapers. After all, stripped of all the politics, the Schiavo case was an end-of-life negotiation that was messy and painful for a family, something he sees all the time. The other case concerned the limits of autonomy and religious rights, and Bowman worried that one reason the coverage was muted was that the media don't seem too interested in stories involving Jehovah's Witnesses, Mormons and others with religious beliefs that aren't in the mainstream. "The problem is we think those religions are wacky and too extreme. Their pamphlets are poorly illustrated and they knock on the door too often and you can't take that seriously." And yet, from a Canadian perspective, Bowman argued, the blood transfusion case was more meaningful than the Schiavo case.

As strongly as he felt about the issues, Bowman remained apprehensive about speaking out in the media. I'd heard a clip of him talking about it on CBC Radio that morning, but he told me when the radio on his alarm came on and he heard his name, he had put a pillow over his radio and thought, "Oh my God, I don't want to hear any of this."

His understandable fear is that he'll get a referral and the patient or family will say, "I saw you on TV and I don't want anything to do with you because you're biased." Or a doctor or nurse or department head might say, "You've already got your own agenda, so why are we bringing you in here? Your mind is already made up before you come in; I've heard you speak." Given that so much of his work involves end-of-life decisions, taking part in CBC Radio's town hall debate on assisted suicide was a huge risk. But caught between Catherine Frazee, the co-director of Ryerson University's Institute for Disability Studies Research and Education, and Svend Robinson, the former NDP MP who had witnessed the assisted suicide of Sue Rodriguez, Bowman was scrupulously even-handed.

Although he's not entirely sure he can navigate the tension between being a clinician and being a public issue ethicist, he wants to give it a try. "I don't know if I can work it out. I'm experimenting with this and moving slowly." Some ethicists believe teaching doesn't stop at the university gates and needs to involve educating more than just students—they also have an obligation to the public because it's a new and emerging profession and the public is curious about these issues. "I am beginning to agree with that," he said, adding that most people at the Joint Centre for Bioethics, even many of the ones who don't do clinical work, don't like dealing with reporters because they are afraid of being tricked or having their words taken out of context. Ethicists generally can't talk about the cases they are involved in, and when they agree to talk about other cases, they're careful to preface their comments with the proviso that they don't know all the details. Too often, though, reporters clip such caveats and the ethicists are left feeling burned.

"They see it as damn high risk," Bowman admitted. Through his ape work, though, he has come to realize that getting misquoted doesn't happen as often as people think. His growing comfort with the media can't reduce the fear of compromising his ability to do clinical work, but he believes the obligation outweighs the risks. "If ethics is what we say it is—a way of thinking and a new language of examining deep social problems and medical problems—then it really can't stay in academic and health circles. It really needs broader exposure."

We talked about this on the deck in my backyard. I'd opened a bottle of white wine and put out a plate of cheese that he attacked with obvious relish. At first, as our discussion wore on, he passed on a second glass of wine, saying he had to go home and continue working on a paper he was preparing for peer review. He'd been working on it all day and he seemed less than enthusiastic about it. Eventually, he grabbed the bottle and poured himself a glass. "I'm increasingly disillusioned with the academic world, and that's not a huge problem, because I have only one foot in it—well, maybe one and a half feet—but writing for peer-reviewed medical or ethical journals, I mean big deal," he said with a laugh. "In the grand scheme of things, what are you doing? Jane Goodall has the right approach. She consciously made her decision long ago to move away from that kind of cloistered world and into the mainstream. And she was right. Writing for peer-reviewed journals about chimp behaviour or even conservation and chimps—to what end? Get out there."

Only a year and a half earlier, as I sat with him in his JCB office, he'd had a starkly different take on the subject. "Doing a lot of clinical work is career suicide. It really is. You see a lot of patients, you do things thoroughly, you make sure you get back and show up at the dying person's bedside and really do proper clinical work," he'd told me, adding that he also wanted to keep publishing articles every year. "The way to move a career is to write and publish. And there are many ethicists who just stay with that and say, 'Ultimately, I'm more effective if I do this, so I will.' They've got a huge strategic advantage. Not that I'm desperately trying to move my career—I'm pretty happy with it as it is—but it's hard."

Clearly, by the fall of 2005, something had changed. He was losing interest in academic work and becoming increasingly attracted to public issue ethics. "I have to be very careful as my career moves toward concepts and opinions and media," he said after we'd talked about assisted suicide. "If I talk like this, I'm going to have a lot of trouble doing clinical work, because people are going to agree or disagree with my position."

If it came down to a choice, would he choose the clinical work?

"Probably. Yeah," he said, but I definitely sensed a hesitation that I'm sure wouldn't have been there before. "Probably. Yeah."

Since then, he's only grown bolder as a public issue ethicist. In fact, in 2008, University of Toronto president David Naylor, a former dean of medicine, told him: "You have moxie with the media." At first, Bowman worried it might be a hint to cool it, but then realized it was a compliment.

WHEN I WAS IN SUDBURY with Bowman, I joined him and some of the Science North staff for dinner. Although he was knowledgeable on a range of subjects, had lots of opinions and was a good storyteller, he didn't play the star attraction and didn't seem to need to be the centre of attention. Still, it would be naive to conclude he doesn't have a strong ego—he's too ambitious and he works too hard for that. Bowman likes to keep busy, and with his responsibilities at the hospital and the JCB, his position as an assistant professor of family and community medicine, speaking engagements, additional teaching gigs, his ape work (which includes public speaking, writing, raising money and travelling to Africa) and trying to fit in a daily swim, staying busy is hardly a problem for him. In fact, he often works seven days a week and usually needs to get up early to get everything done. Even then it's a challenge. He frequently complains that he can't keep up with his email. One time I was on the phone with him and he was trying, unsuccessfully, to find some information he wanted to give me when suddenly he blurted out in exasperation: "I have 162 emails on my server and most of them haven't been opened." He tries to keep most of his ape work to weekends, but during a typical day the two careers inevitably blend. He gets five weeks vacation and often devotes much of that time to African trips. He's also taken part in two documentaries— *Bushmeat* and one that appeared on CBC's *The Nature of Things*—and has tried to sell filmmakers on others. In another connection between bioethics and his conservation work, he tried to convince a filmmaker to make a documentary on the global health issue of retroviruses, pointing out that HIV likely first transferred to humans because people ate chimpanzee bushmeat, that the SARS outbreak that hit Toronto in 2003 probably originated from civet cats sold in markets in China, and that avian flu is carried by poultry and other birds. Meanwhile, Jane Goodall has encouraged him to write a book.

Along with two careers, Bowman has two offices a couple of blocks apart—one at Mount Sinai and the other on the second floor of the JCB. The latter is cramped and cluttered and filled with all the telltale signs of an overworked occupant, including stacks of papers and reports. There's also a large yucca tree in the corner. He found it in the garbage, nursed it back to health and revels in its smell when it flowers. At home he makes room for rabbits, chinchillas and an antique tortoise that came to Canada in 1938 and has lived with him since 1974. His devotion to animals might seem at odds with his hard-working, if not hard-driving, side. This is, after all, a man who juggles his conservation calling with his clinical work and his academic position—and sometimes teaches a night course at York University. He may not fit the mould of the workaholic careerist, and yet he obviously has ambitions—not just to save the apes (a cause as much as an ambition, I suppose) but also as a clinical ethicist.

AT THE END of one of my meetings with Bowman, I had to ask him about the word "Mindfulness" written on a Post-it note above his desk. I'd been wondering about it for an hour and a half.

"Mindfulness. It's a Buddhist concept that is really a way of just trying to stay in the present and focused and remain calm. Buddhists talk a lot about the Western mind and the Eastern mind," he explained. "All senses are essentially pointed outwards. At all times. From a Buddhist perspective, their senses are reversed and they're pointed inward. 'How am I doing?' Not in a self-involved way, but 'How am I breathing? How uptight am I? Am I staying in the moment? Am I perceptive?' And we're out there, scrambling. So Mindfulness is a way of turning this focus the other way."

He'd put it up there six months earlier, and while he admitted that he sometimes stopped noticing it, the little yellow reminder had helped him.

"Are you a Buddhist?" I asked him.

"I'm interested in Buddhism. Very much so. Increasingly so. Mindfulness to me means take a deep breath, pull yourself right back to the moment. It's very grounding, very focused. If you do it often enough, and gently enough, it actually starts to work after a while. If you stay in the present, mostly, you're way more effective at whatever you're doing. But the Western mind ... well, you can see where I'm going. I've got this meeting, I'm pushing my day ahead. And it's not a good thing to do because if you're going to do anything well and really enjoy the moment, you've got to stay put. But most of these Buddhists don't have the bloody, frantic schedules we have. I'd love to see them on cellphones and with all these responsibilities. I wonder if they'd unravel."

6 Finding Serenity
Five brothers try to ensure their mother feels no pain

BY THE TIME Peter hit his mid-thirties, he'd seen more death than many people see in a lifetime. But that and the help of his four brothers didn't make watching his mother die any easier, especially since, in the end, they had to hasten the process. Here is the story he told me.

My parents died twelve years and ten feet apart. My father died in his bed in 1984 and my mother died in her bed in 1996. When my father died it was all new, and he died at home and I was there throughout his illness. He was diagnosed in 1983 and liver cancer is basically untreatable, but he didn't have a messy cancer, so we were able to look after his personal needs at home.

One day, my brother Brad couldn't understand what he was saying. My father was lying in his bed with his hands like this [he mimed someone at the wheel of a car] ... but he was only speaking in a whisper. So Brad called my mother, and she couldn't understand what he was saying, so she called me. He was saying he wanted to go home. With his hands, he was driving. I looked at my mother and said, "He wants to go home."

Right away she said, "Harry, I think that's a wonderful idea. You should go home." And she started listing off all the people he would see, people who were all already dead. There's an element of permission and release involved, and he went into a coma and died the next night.

When he died, we called the funeral home, and they were all wearing black and they all looked like ghouls. My mother and I were in the room and they said, "You might want to leave." They were going to put him in a body bag, and it was going to be unpleasant because of things that happen to the body when it dies. And we said no. We'd seen it all. It was unpleasant, but we weren't going to turn our eyes from reality.

There was a certain fascination for me, as well, because when someone is pregnant we all do the laying of hands on the belly and everybody's involved in the pregnancy and we find out about epidurals and how many centimetres she was dilated before and whether she had to have an episiotomy and all this stuff. We hear every single detail now. But nobody talks about the process of dying, and it's as intimate a thing as birth and it happens to all of us. If we were born, we're going to die. But we don't talk about it. We do turn our eyes from it.

I think my father's death was one of the most difficult but amazing experiences for me. He taught me a great deal, because he and I hadn't gotten along for many years before he died. And once he found out he was ill, he mended his bridges. It was a wake-up call to him to do something. My father was fifty-eight when he died and I was twenty-two and we became fast friends during the course of his illness.

And then, after that, a lot of friends of mine were dying. So, unfortunately, I had an early exposure to death. I mean, I'm a gay man of a certain age. I worked as a buddy from 1986 to 1990. It was a volunteer thing. When people—including medical people—were so terrified of anyone with AIDS, we gave personal assistance to these people, social assistance when they were at home or visiting and being their advocate in hospitals. They were strangers, but they were in need.

And so I wasn't unused to the process; I was quite familiar with it. I had a chum whose best friend had AIDS, and they had made a pact that when he would have difficulty walking he was going to commit suicide, and it was interesting to see, because he kept moving the goal posts. He kept on pushing back what the thing that he couldn't live with would be. He got Kaposi's [Kaposi's sarcoma is a type of cancer often associated with AIDS] on the bottoms of his feet and had a horrible time walking. But he could live with that. Then he said, "If I should be facially scarred with Kaposi's …" and that started happening. Then he found himself more socially isolated and his life became miserable—indoors and everything was hard. So that's when he decided he didn't want to do it anymore. When he finally decided that he'd had enough, his doctor let him know—wink-wink, nudge-nudge—"If you take this many of this pill, it will kill you."

My mother was very social. She loved to sit with people of every generation and really talk and really listen. Talk and talk and talk. She was a great mother. She looked after it all—she ran the household within an inch of its life, she looked after her husband, she looked after her children, these five big galoots who could barely pick their own noses. And she was very beautiful. She had great legs, she had a great bosom and she had a beautiful face. Even when she was diminished and ill, she filled the place with a certain colour and spirit and a sense of the way things should be done.

She had been feeling poorly for some time and had been going to all kinds of doctors to find out what the problem was. In May of 1996, the doctor said, "All your tests have come back and on paper you're as healthy as a horse. But I believe you when you say you feel ill. So come back next week and we'll start all over again and we'll find out what the matter is. But don't worry, because it's not cancer."

So she went back on a day that I was in Ottawa. When I came home the next day, she said, "Sit down, I have to talk to you." I sat down and she said, "I have cancer." She'd gone to the doctor, and he told her that he'd spoken too soon, that there was one test they'd done that he didn't have the results from when he'd spoken to her a week prior, and that was the bone scan, and indeed she did have cancer. And he cried and he apologized.

She said to the doctor right away—and set the tone right away—she said to the doctor, "I'm not interested in pursuing any treatment. I've seen too many people go through it and I'm not a young person anymore. If I was a thirty-five-year-old mother perhaps, but I'm sixty-five years old. So all I want to do is make a deal with you, right now. No pain." And they shook on it.

I felt very guilty, because I'd never been away. I felt so badly that I wasn't there for her to come home to for comfort. I said, "What did you do?" She said, "I came home and I made an appointment to have my hair done and my streaks done, which I'm doing tomorrow, and afterwards you're going to meet me, because we're going to go down the street and pick out new eyeglasses, because I think I'm going to be losing some weight."

So the tone was set: this is happening and we're going to deal with it. And we did.

She went into hospital soon thereafter to have a palliative procedure whereby they put a steel bar into her hip. And then I had to go to Toronto for work for a month, but she was in the hospital the whole time. When I got back I went home to an empty house, because she was being brought home the next day by ambulance. She was in a wheelchair because of her hip, and we lived in an upper duplex, so it was going to be an ordeal getting her up the stairs.

That was the one moment I regret the most, because I hadn't seen her for a month. The doorbell rang and there she was, sitting on the front step in a wheelchair with this orderly behind her, and she had the look of death on her—a hollow-ness of the cheeks but particularly a hollowness under the chin. And I opened that door and I couldn't help myself; I hadn't seen her for a month, and I saw it and it flashed on my face, very quickly, but she saw it flash on my face. She was so happy to see me again and come home again, and it was in a flash, but it told her she was dying. And even though we knew this, because she wasn't pursuing treatment, it was still hard to come to terms with. That was the hardest moment, of the whole thing [his eyes filled with tears and he took several seconds before continuing] … But she came in and we got on with it.

Now, unfortunately, within thirty-six hours she would be in Emergency. She had this terrible pain—terrible, terrible, terrible pain—and we were back and forth between her bed and the bathroom all night long. We were still sorting out the medication and so on, and she had been given this steroid. It was a very, very long night, and finally in the morning I called her doctor and he said, "Call an ambulance. Get her to hospital right away."

When a 911 call like that goes out, for some reason they also send a fire truck, and all these firemen came into the house and went into her bathroom. And they were all suited up with the helmets on and the boots and everything, and my mother was sitting in the bathroom just in terrible pain and the fireman said to her, "Don't worry, ma'am, you can swear if you want to. We're firemen."

When we arrived at the hospital, the ambulance paramedic pulled me aside and said, "What have they told you about this? This is a very, very sick woman and don't you let them not tell you. I'm a paramedic, and my mother died earlier this year and they didn't tell me a thing. This woman is very ill."

It turned out that because of the steroid her bowel had ruptured. And they were going to have to do immediate surgery. I was with her in the hallway before she was wheeled into an operating room. She had the cap and gown on and everything. And she said, "Well, Peter, at least you got to meet some firemen." Because she knows the particular affinity I have.

I told her this wasn't her time. She was going to die, but this was too soon, too much needed to be done beforehand, and she had to pull through this. I believed that. She hadn't said goodbye yet to people, myself included. She was going to die of cancer—not an aneurysm or a heart attack or a rupture—and that was going to be a process.

I went home and I lost my mind. I literally was out of my mind. Her bed had been thrashed and it was a mess, and she was very particular about everything, always being very neat and tidy. And she loved her bed. So I stripped the bed and made it about four or five times as a bargain that, if it was made perfectly, she would survive and she would come home. If that bed wasn't perfect, I stripped the whole thing and made it again and made it again and made it again. Those corners had to be so perfect, and everything had to be so perfect, and if it was, she would come home and sleep in it again.

Finally, I got a hold of myself and came back to earth.

It's just shocking what the body can do to itself in the last stages. And the thing that drives you crazy about these kinds of illnesses is how they strip you of any dignity and each little bit goes. Suddenly, she had to lay herself bare and let somebody look after her colostomy bag. She would always apologize, "I'm so sorry. I'm so sorry. I'm so sorry." And I said, "Look, you wiped my ass for how many years? I was pukin' and shittin' all over the place as a little kid; this is the least I can do." She was in a diminished situation and I was in my hale and hardy years. It was not a problem. It didn't bother me with my mother or my father.

There was a point at which she had a bit of a crisis. It was a Friday in August and the doctor had come over, and he said, "I think you should get your family here. I don't think she'll die tonight, but I don't think she'll make it through the weekend." They all came home, but she didn't die. The house was full and it was quite something. All of a sudden she was this sun, and her five favourite planets were orbiting around her. She wasn't going to leave.

It started becoming more difficult. We got a hospital bed in. She had been taking morphine in pill form, and then that stopped working because she wasn't swallowing and she wasn't really producing enough spit for it to dissolve under her tongue. So then they started putting morphine patches on her, but that wasn't working because you need a layer of flesh and fat underneath and she was just skin and bone. So they put in a tube for injections and gave us two things to inject her with— one was morphine and the other was a drug to clear the lungs, because she was having trouble breathing.

There were only two pharmacies in Montreal that would keep morphine on the premises. All the rest would order it for you, but it would be a twenty-four-hour wait. Fortunately, one of them was nearby, and so we'd go, but we wouldn't send just one person to collect it, because we were afraid he would be hit on the head on the way out. So two or three of us would go, and over the course of that ten days, when she was needing more and more, the head pharmacist would be the only one to dispense it. At our third visit, he looked at us and said, "Guys, sorry to ask this, but she's still alive?"

One of the nurses said that on the same day my mother started her morphine they had another patient who had started morphine at five milligrams, and the patient died that night and the family was up in arms. The family accused them of euthanizing this person. They told me, "It goes either way and you can never predict, but morphine has become your mother's friend." It had become her sustenance. She was doing like a hundred and something milligrams at a time. They said this happens sometimes, and I think between that and wanting to be around for the party, so to speak—in the sense that all her boys were there staring at her and hanging on her every word, which had never happened prior to that—she didn't want to go. And morphine had given her this sort of backbone to stick around.

One day one of my brothers came running and said, "Come, come. Hurry. She wants a martini and a cigarette." It was like eleven o'clock in the morning, and I was so happy, because when illness comes you don't know in life when's the last time you're going to have sex, when's the last time you're going to have a cigarette, when's the last time you're going to have a drink. You don't know, but this might be the last one. I was so glad, because she had been through the mill and this was the last week of her life and she decided she was going to have a cigarette and a martini, and so I made a martini and went into the room and she took a sip. Here she is, packed up with morphine, and she takes a sip of the martini and goes, "Whoa." She hadn't had booze in so long. And then she said, "You light the cigarette." I lit the cigarette and put it to her lips and she did the big inhale and then, just like a stoner, she goes, "Whoooaaa."

We all had those great little experiences in the last days, but it just got beyond the point. It was just pathetic to watch her and to put yourself in her shoes, to think you're just lying there, wracked with the most unbearable pain all day. And yet she wouldn't go.

With the morphine, she'd have these odd hallucinations. She saw the stereotypical pink elephants. And fire. Fire was a terrible thing, and she would get in a real panic. Just like my father wanted to drive home, my mother would pick up an invisible phone and start talking to people and tell them that her bags were packed and she would see them in a bit, she was coming. And we realized that everybody she was talking to was already dead.

Somebody was in the room with her twenty-four hours a day. And I think that was important because she had private time with each of us and was able to say goodbye to each of us. And so she didn't die until she was ready to.

But after seeing all the effect of my brothers, I said to them, "Listen, I'm closing the door on the bedroom and I'm spending the day with her alone. None of you are to come in."

They said fine. They knew this was now getting to be a problem, because she wasn't eating, she was in terrible pain and it was getting hard to look after her because you couldn't touch her. By the time she died, the cancer had eaten through bone all over her and to touch her or move her or roll her over was impossible. So I sat with her for the day and she was in and out. I counted her breaths and took her pulse. Her breaths were very laboured and heavy.

I said, "You know I will do anything for you, you know that. I will do anything for you, but there's one thing you're going to have to do for yourself, which I can't do, and that's to let go." We'd all given her permission to let go.

And she said, "I know, I know, I know."

I said, "I know you can see the other side, I know you can see it, and you're just going to have to make that step. I can't do it for you, though I would."

"I know, I know, I know."

Finally, this one nurse came, and she said she'd spoken to a friend of hers who was a doctor at an AIDS hospice on the south shore of Montreal. She told him about my mother's condition, about the fact that morphine was sustaining her and that she should have been dead a week prior. And he said that he'd seen this as well and that what they did was use a drug called Versed and that this "helps." The doctor called that same pharmacy and put in a prescription. This other nurse was going to come on Saturday to administer it, because she'd had some experience with it before and it has to be administered in a very particular way. It's a very slow injection.

So here's this drug, and I'm reading the box and it's very frank that it's a one-off, whereas the prescription was "Use as needed." So there's a bit of a dilemma there. Rick, Brad, Derek and I were there, Saturday morning, and Phil was at home. The nurse came in and I said, "Listen, we're having a bit of a disconnect here. The box says this and the prescription says that and I don't understand the difference. What does 'as needed' mean?"

She just said, "Ach, that's very delicate" [he said this in a thick Scottish burr].

Then the doorbell rang, and who should come in

unannounced but the doctor. And I said, "You wrote a prescription 'as needed.' What does that mean?"

"Well, if she's not serene."

That was so brilliant. What a beautiful word, and that was what we were all trying to work toward in her care—that she be serene—and that was the deal she made with him at the outset: no pain.

But we were a group of boys, and boys aren't very good about talking about these things. So I said, "Before you go ahead, we have to talk." I went into another room with my brothers to be frank about what we were doing and should we proceed. Brad had been there for a number of days and he and I were on the same page, and we said, "We pledged to her that we would take care of her and this is taking care of her. You can't touch her because she's in such pain. She's not living, she's not eating, she's barely drinking, she's in and out of consciousness. This is taking care of her."

I don't know that we were frank in the sense of saying, "We're killing her here," but frank in the sense of we had to stop and take a measured response to what we're possibly going to do. And I said, "We're a bunch of boys, we'll probably never talk about this again, so let's make sure we're all all right with this and everybody's on the same page. Don't let events whip you up and take you along; you have a say in this—though if you object, I'm going to argue with you."

Rick and Derek were there too, they saw what was going on. I don't know if they were entirely comfortable with it, but the logic was there. They didn't voice any objections, but I don't know that they were enthusiastic. They recognized that it was the only way to go. There weren't a lot of other options. She was just this body, wracked with cancer, riddled with pain, in and out of lucidity. She wasn't communicating much anymore.

She wasn't leading a life of any sort. And as Brad and I said, "We pledged to take care of her, and it's beyond the point now where to make a meal or put a facecloth on her face is doing her any good."

Because of my experience with death, I think it was easier to look at it boldly and in the face, but it wasn't an easy thing to do. Even looking at that poor person lying in the bed, nobody wanted her to be dead. But she wasn't living anymore, so we recognized that she had to be put out of her misery.

We went back and said, "Okay, go ahead."

The nurse administered it and showed us how it was done. Then Brad and I went and got her an orchid, and when we came home it was evening time and she was awake and kind of alert-looking in the eyes. She wasn't really talking or anything. She saw the orchid and her eyes lit up.

Later that night, she started moaning in pain again and she was still sort of out of it, but moaning. So we gave her another shot. And then she slept a great deal. Then she got another shot the next night. And Brad slept right on the floor beside her bed that night. And at around five o'clock Monday morning he came in and roused me and said, "She's gone."

We knew what we wanted. There was trepidation. It's such a grey zone, but you had the tacit approval of the medical authorities—actually, the provision of the means by the medical authorities—and a decision to be made within the family about how to proceed. I think everybody recognized that it was the proper course. It might not have been the desired course, but only in a selfish way. You want the person still around. But she wasn't going to get better.

I don't regret anything that we did, but it wasn't easy. We all wish that she would have died naturally—on her own steam, so to speak. But that wasn't happening and that's why it needed an intervention. We didn't pump her up with the stuff—we took the cue of "not serene." The minute there was clearly pain, we gave it to her, but with the understanding from the indications and warnings on the box that this shouldn't be done.

I'm not keen on euthanasia, but I would be keen on assistance, whereby it helped you along but it didn't kill you. It's done all the time in hospitals, where you up either the dose or the repetition of morphine. Things like that I'm very comfortable with, because it seems to me you're not completely intervening with the course of life by stopping it, but you're hastening it.

So, ethically, I think I like to remain in the grey zone. I can live with that, knowing that we didn't put a pillow over her head, so to speak. We just took away whatever it was that just kept her going way beyond her point, to allow the process to unfold the way it should have. Now that was through conscious intervention. We were well apprised of what we were doing—or not necessarily well apprised, because nobody could talk about it, but we knew what we were doing, and in my mind it needed to be done. And I don't regret any of that at all, at all, at all. I don't have any guilt or regret at all.

I didn't want my brothers all to go into their four different corners and feel as though maybe decisions were made that they were not entirely happy with or clear about. We had to be clear about what we were doing. And really it's come to pass— we haven't really talked about it since. I think everybody has a very private feeling about it, but personally I was vocal about it, and I still feel it was the right thing to do.

A lot of my memories are of that three-month period and some of them are horrible. I try to put them aside, but it's not always easy—they occur without my expecting it. A lot of those have started to fade over time, but those three months have an undue weight in my memory. I'm stuck there. It's long-term grief.

People now come to me as their parents are getting older and sick and are facing death. "What should I expect? What should I do? How should I talk to them?" Because they know I've been through it. And while I encourage everybody to get as involved as possible, I don't say it lightly. I know that it has consequences. You're going to remember things that are not pleasant, you're going to have experiences that are debilitating in many ways. But I think the option of relegating it to somebody else is worse.

In many, many cases, people are not willing to put their lives aside or confront the realities of it. They'll leave it up to so-called professionals. You don't have to be a professional; mostly it's pain management. And you can get palliative care at home and you can learn how to administer the medication. You also know the ebbs and flows of the person throughout the day and when their pain management should be upped and when they need their medication better than a harried nurse. You're completely on top of things. I learned about output of urine, breaths per minute, heartbeats per minute—those things where you will not die above a certain threshold, but if it goes below a certain threshold you're into the shutdown of organs. You learn all those things and you have to be willing to ask the questions.

From the palliative care nurses who looked after my mother, I heard terrible stories about people. In one case, this nurse came in shaking her head because she'd just been to this patient who was an old man living at his family's, and she said they were all up at the front of the house smoking cigarettes and playing cards and he was lying in the bed at the back of the house. They weren't paying him any attention; they were just, "Let him die."

So, get as involved as possible. The finality of death is so hard to figure out if you haven't confronted it before. But once they're gone, if you have a regret, there's no fixing it. I just tell people: let them die without any regrets on your part, because you're the one who is going to be left behind, and it's no good if you have to beat yourself up afterwards—"I should have done this; I should have done that; I should have been more present; I should have been more involved."

If you have the capacity and the time to be involved, do. Throw everything away and just tell everybody else, "I'm putting you on hold." This is real life at its most stark and it's very challenging, but once it's over, it is so over that, if you have any regrets about it, you can't fix them afterwards. And the industrialization of death by sending somebody off to hospital and waiting for a phone call, I think is incredibly unnatural and creates an unnecessary mystery and unnecessary guilt afterwards.

By mucking in and rolling up your sleeves and getting involved in the deaths of your parents, it demystifies something that is completely natural and is going to happen to all of us. And you don't have regrets at the end. You can say to yourself at the funeral that you did everything that you could do.

Unlike an aneurysm or a heart attack, an illness affords you the opportunity to mend your bridges, which is what my father did. You have choices to make and suddenly you behave in a different way, you speak to people in a different way. And people can speak to you in a different way. And that's why I say it's an opportunity and why people should get involved.

7 The Conversation

Why writing a living will isn't a substitute for talking about death

TERRI SCHIAVO made the feeding tube famous. In 1990, the twenty-six-year-old Florida woman's heart stopped, depriving her of oxygen long enough to cause severe brain damage. Doctors later discovered that the cause of her cardiac arrest had been a potassium deficiency, which may have been caused by bulimia (as a teenager Schiavo had weighed as much as 250 pounds, but was down to 110). Her collapse put her in a persistent vegetative state with no hope of improvement. She stayed alive with the help of a feeding tube that entered her stomach through a hole in her abdomen, and her internal organs continued to function even though her brain—except for the stem, which controls breathing, digestion and other involuntary functions—was dead. Like most people, Schiavo had not prepared a living will. Initially, her husband, Michael, whom the courts appointed as her guardian, and her parents, Robert and Mary Schindler, agreed that the doctors should do whatever it took to keep her alive. But in 1998, Michael changed his mind, claiming that Terri had said she would never want to be kept alive if she were in that position, and filed a petition to remove the feeding tube. Soon her private tragedy landed in the courts, was covered with macabre zeal by the media and became tangled up in America's wacky abortion politics as the religious right—

fresh from a string of political victories, including the re-election of a president who was a born-again Christian—eagerly turned Schiavo into a martyr for their movement.

By January 2005, the case had reached the U.S. Supreme Court, which refused to consider it. Then things started to get really nutty: while the Schindlers continued to explore every possible legal avenue to keep their daughter alive, anti-abortion activists joined the fray, a Florida businessman offered Michael a million dollars to withdraw his request to have Terri's feeding tube removed, and politicians seized the opportunity to cater to a powerful constituency. The Senate delayed its Easter recess and worked through the night to pass a bill that applied only to Schiavo, while the House of Representatives cut its Easter break short for a special session to debate the law (in other words, U.S. politicians were willing to do more for one woman who had been brain dead for fifteen years than they were for the millions of people killed in various genocides and atrocities around the world). Meanwhile, some individual politicians outdid themselves. Perhaps the most egregious example came from House majority leader Tom DeLay. The Texan—who had owned a successful pest control business before he went into politics—offered his own medical assessment: "Terri Schiavo is not brain dead; she talks and she laughs, and she expresses happiness and discomfort. Terri Schiavo is not on life support." He also denounced Michael Schiavo—and the judiciary—for "an act of barbarism." Even by the low standards of the modern politician, it seemed a particularly shameless attack because in 1998, DeLay and his family had opted to take his own father off life support and allow him to die.

Protesters mounted a death watch outside the hospital, and on March 31, 2005, thirteen days after doctors removed the feeding tube for the third and final time, Schiavo died, though the political exploitation of her did not.

By this time, Kerry Bowman had started gingerly adding media work to his repertoire and had already earned a reputation as a good interview. But he was out of the country, travelling in Africa and Iran, so he couldn't respond to the many requests to comment that were clogging his voice mail. After he returned, I asked him for his take. "I think that one of the reasons it evoked such passionate outrage in people is that it suddenly dawned on them that, 'Oh my God, are we doing this all the time?'" he said. "The answer is yes, we're negotiating end-of-life decisions every single day. And not a couple across the country, but in every one of our hospitals and nursing homes and everything else. Day in and day out. They just don't all blow up."

The battle between Schiavo's parents and her husband didn't strike Bowman as newsworthy. Most families reach some consensus—though it sometimes requires a little gentle nudging or mediation from a hospital ethicist—rather than fighting it out in the courts or on television, but plenty of them do battle. There's nothing like the stress of watching someone die for bringing all the family baggage out in the open. "Families fighting over end of life? Have I ever seen that? I earn my income that way. It sounds horrible, but I do. I see that endlessly."

He also pointed out that doctors regularly withdraw life-sustaining treatments, including antibiotics, ventilators, dialysis and even pacemakers. I suggested that while some people were appalled that doctors could remove a feeding tube, others were dismayed that doctors would keep someone alive in that condition for fifteen years. "We are," Bowman said matter-of-factly, "doing that too."

THE FEEDING TUBE is just one of many medical advances that allow doctors to keep patients alive longer. But such technology was never developed to sustain patients for years and years. Yes, doctors have an obligation to do everything for their patients, but the problem is that not everyone agrees on what "everything" is. In the past it wasn't much. But now, when so much is possible, it means different things to different people: Do we return a dying patient to the operating room for a fourth time? Should someone get a second heart transplant when many other people are waiting for their first? Should we hook a severely brain-damaged young woman up to a feeding tube indefinitely? Surely it's some reasonable quality of life, not biology, that we want to maintain. And yet "quality of life" is something else for which we all have different definitions.

For my generation, the Schiavo debacle was an eerie reminder of the case of Karen Ann Quinlan, which was a seminal chapter in the history of the right-to-die movement. In 1975, the twenty-one-year-old New Jersey woman collapsed at a party, apparently after mixing gin and barbiturates. She ended up in a persistent vegetative state. Once it became clear that she would never recover, her devoutly Catholic family—keenly aware that their daughter had been an active and athletic person—asked doctors to remove her from the respirator. The Quinlans did not want the medical team to take any extraordinary measures to keep her alive, and they even had the support of their parish priest. But the hospital refused. When the Quinlans won in New Jersey's Supreme Court, the doctors finally followed the family's wishes, removing the respirator, though not the feeding tube. But Karen Ann kept breathing and survived until 1985, when she died of pneumonia in a nursing home.

The media attention this story attracted, although tame in comparison to the wall-to-wall Schiavo hysteria, prompted a lot of people to think about how we die, in many cases for the first time. And along with the legal precedent the Quinlan case set, it also led to the establishment of ethics committees in some hospitals and the development of living wills.

Years later, though, living wills still weren't well understood. One day, I ran into an old friend whose father's second wife was in a coma. The prognosis was far from good, but the woman kept hanging on. My friend knew her stepmother had written a living will and stored it away somewhere, and now seemed like the right time for the family to take a look at it. But when she called her stepbrother—who apparently didn't know what a living will was, let alone that his mother had one—he became angry and upset and accused my friend of worrying more about what she would inherit than about the health of his mother.

That encounter was a year or two before the Schiavo case educated so many about living wills. In 2006, Mary Wohlford, an eighty-year-old retired nurse living in Dyersville, Iowa, was so appalled by the Schiavos' fate that she signed a living will, talked to her family about it and hung it on her refrigerator. Then, to make sure there could be no confusion, she went to a tattoo parlour and had "Do not resuscitate" tattooed on her chest. "People might think I'm crazy, but that's OK," she told the *Des Moines Register*. "Sometimes the nuttiest ideas are the most advanced."

Living wills are designed to solve many end-of-life disputes and make decisions less painful for family members. These documents set out what care and treatment people want and don't want, in case they're ever unable to communicate their wishes for themselves. Living wills—which go by different names (including advanced directive, personal directive or power of attorney for personal care) and have different powers depending on the province—are designed to help next of kin and doctors make decisions on a patient's behalf. In an end-of-life case, the question, legally and ethically in Canada, is not, "What do you want to do for your husband?" It is, or is supposed to be, "If your husband could speak for himself, what would he ask us to do?" So even if a wife believes continued aggressive treatment is the only right thing to do, but actually knows her husband wouldn't want it, then the only right answer is, "I think my husband would want the plug pulled."

PETER SINGER'S OFFICE at the Joint Centre for Bioethics was big enough that the clutter—including stacks of binders, papers and reports on the floor—didn't seem overwhelming at all. I was sitting across from him at a small conference table when a woman knocked on the door and told him it was time to go. Short and squat, Singer wore a dark blue tie with little University of Toronto insignias on it. He put on a white doctor's coat and then an overcoat and walked briskly in his beat-up burgundy loafers out of the old church that's home to the JCB and half a block over to Toronto General Hospital, where a public relations woman and Jenny Manzer, a writer and photographer from the *Medical Post*, were waiting for him in the lobby. The publication wanted a picture of him for a story about an academic paper Singer and his colleagues had written for the *Annals of Internal Medicine* that proposed a Limited Aggressive Therapy Order, which would offer a middle ground between Do Not Resuscitate orders and blanket resuscitation instructions. As he moved through the hospital, several doctors and nurses said hello, and in the elevator he chatted in an easy way with two women he clearly knew.

On the ninth-floor cardiac ward, the entourage found a defibrillator and wheeled it down the hall. As Manzer took shots with her old Pentax, Singer held the paddles above an imaginary patient. As JCB director, he knew that working with the media was part of the job; in fact, he said that the centre should be a public resource for information on bioethics and even arranged media training for the ethicists. But he looked more than a little self-conscious holding the defibrillator paddles against an imaginary body for a photo op. When Manzer asked him to try to look sombre, he couldn't quite get the nervous smile from his face. So Manzer moved around to take advantage of another angle, but as she continued clicking away she noticed the sign in the background. "That Exit sign is—" she started.

But he finished her sentence: "a bit ominous."

He relaxed a bit after that. After all, Singer may not be that comfortable with the media, but he knows a lot about the way people exit. Although his particular interest these days is global health inequities, he devoted much of the early part of his career to trying to improve end-of-life care.

Somehow we've let all our technology and medical know-how make dying worse, rather than better. Earlier generations tended to die at home, and if there was a doctor around, there probably wasn't much he could do to speed up or slow down the inevitable. "Sixty or eighty years ago, people would die in their living rooms," said Singer. "They'd be surrounded by their families and they be comforted. The doctor might visit and prescribe as much morphine as needed, and there was a close personal bond. I'm probably idealizing a bit, but people at least died in a socially supported circumstance." By the 1970s and 1980s, with the increasing institutionalization of death in hospitals, that was no longer true. "Death changed, and it wasn't pretty," he said. "Now everyone has a horror story about a loved one who died. It might be a loved one who died in pain; it might be a loved one hooked up to a machine and nobody asked him whether he wanted it or not; it might be a loved one who died alone in a nursing home. It doesn't have to be that way."

Singer first became interested in the subject in 1978, when he was a student at Upper Canada College—a private school for boys in Toronto—and a science teacher assigned him an essay on human-subject experimentation. He went on to med school at U of T assuming that he'd not only learn more about such issues in his classes but also discuss them with classmates and professors. He was shocked to find out that wasn't the case. Back then, the few classes in bioethics at the university were so philosophical and theoretical that they didn't have much to do with the care of patients. So, with a group of colleagues, Singer organized a series of seminars on bioethics. His decision to devote his career to ethics came in 1984 when he was an intern caring for a woman dying of cancer. She was in her thirties and had a low phosphorous level in her blood. "It was a very moving experience for someone who was twenty-four or twenty-five years old," he told me, because he realized he could rattle off twenty medical reasons why someone might have a low phosphorous level, but when it came to whether they were going to resuscitate her when her heart stopped, as it inevitably would, doctors would write instructions in pencil on the nursing orders and then rub them out afterward. "There was no systematic thought given to that side of it." Singer was dismayed that the hospital approached low phosphorous levels in blood with more rigour than it approached death—or what he later began to understand as quality end-of-life care. He saw an opportunity to develop and clarify a set of practices and policies that would lead to better deaths for patients. After studying clinical ethics at the University of Chicago and epidemiology at Yale, he returned to Toronto to work in end-of-life care. He joined U of T's Centre for Bioethics, which became the Joint Centre for Bioethics in 1995 after the centre formed a partnership with eight teaching hospitals (since increased to fifteen health care institutions.) The partnership means the JCB, which is committed to research, teaching, clinical work and acting as a public resource, can focus both on theory and practice.

Singer, who left the JCB in 2006 to join the McLaughlin-Rotman Centre for Global Health, was an ideal leader for the centre. Intelligent, ambitious and driven, he had a vision for the place and, perhaps best of all, was good at raising money, which was crucial to success. But he also had a reputation for smugness, or even arrogance, and his decision to take money from an insurance company—he held the Sun Life Financial Chair in Bioethics—did not go over well with some of his colleagues, who thought that even if there was no conflict of interest, the decision sent the wrong message. Despite that controversy, the centre thrived and now has 215 members, including 30 full-time clinical bioethicists, making it the largest such group in the world.

Singer is especially proud of the living will he developed as JCB director and put on the centre's website. Even before Schiavo, more than a hundred thousand Canadians had used it as a tool to discuss what life-sustaining treatment they wished to receive. For each of several possible states (including stroke, coma and terminal illness) and seven treatments—CPR, ventilator, dialysis, life-saving surgery, blood transfusion, life-saving antibiotics and tube feeding—it allows a choice of four options: yes, no, undecided and trial. The "trial" option means doctors would try a treatment but then stop it if it wasn't making a difference. There's also space for writing additional instructions.

Singer discovered how well it can work, under the right circumstances, when his own mother was sick. She almost died, and he was faced with several questions: Should she have antibiotics? Should she have surgery? Should she go to an intensive care unit? Should she be resuscitated with cardio-pulmonary resuscitation? But she'd filled out one of the JCB's living wills and they had talked about it. "It really gave me peace of mind knowing that even though she couldn't participate in those decisions, I was making decisions that she would have wanted made."

Still, not all experts are as keen on living wills. For one thing, healthy, active people, especially if they're young, can't imagine how anyone could have any kind of quality of life hooked up to a machine, but those that end up in that predicament often find they don't want to give up. I hear plenty of friends say they want to die when they get to the point where someone has to wipe their butts. But as Bowman pointed out, "Lots of people are wiped and fed and toileted. You don't know until you're there."

ARTHUR WAS A BUSINESSMAN in his late fifties. A classic A-type personality, he was a workaholic who ran his own company as well as an insomniac and someone who could never relax. He repeatedly told both his wife and his business partner, "If anything ever happens to me, do me in. Don't ever let me live."

Then, one day, he had a brain-stem stroke. He was breathing on his own, so he wasn't on life support, but he needed a lot of cardiac medication because he'd also suffered a damaging heart attack. When he tried to speak, his words disintegrated into slurring. He was completely out of it. And yet his wife, Claire, had never seen him looking so content: suddenly, he was a gentle, peaceful guy who would happily look at the flowers and the sun and the birds. He even looked different because his face had gone from clenched to calm.

Claire was left with a terrible choice. She could honour his wishes and ask the doctors to stop giving Arthur the heart medication, which would likely send him into arrhythmia, leading to cardiac arrest and death. Or she could refuse to act on his request and let him continue living in his new bliss. As Bowman put it to me: "Philosophically, do you have a stranger (meaning the pre-stroke man) making a decision for essentially a stranger (the relaxed, gentle person) who—one could argue, we don't know this for sure—may be enjoying some of the happiest years of his life? If I, God forbid, had a massive brain-stem stroke and I was sitting in a wheelchair, sitting in front of a window and just staring at beautiful flowers, am I really the same person?"

In the end, Claire left Arthur on the medication, but she was torn apart by her decision because she felt she was breaking her promise to him.

Such radical personality changes are rare, but most of us still find it difficult to imagine what state we'll be in when it comes time for a family member to dig out our living will from the back of the desk drawer. The problem is that living wills can't account for every scenario. Most of them are just standard forms, but there are so many possibilities in medicine that a living will can't capture every single potential brand of misery or altered circumstances we might find ourselves in. Even a phrase in a living will as simple as "reasonable chance of recovery," isn't so simple: after all, what does "reasonable" mean? Few people know what the medical jargon means—and, frankly, most of us wouldn't want to know, because so much of what it covers is just too gruesome to think about. "Living wills are meant to protect the autonomy of a person in a state of incapacity," argued Bowman, "yet you don't know what the details are ahead of time. So, in fact, they're almost the opposite of autonomous choices."

For all these reasons, living wills too often don't work. A better solution is for people to discuss death with each other. That means health care workers and patients have to talk when there's any possibility of someone losing consciousness and declining. These conversations happen more than they used to, but still not often enough. Most of all, though, it means people must understand the values of their loved ones. In Singer's mother's case, for example, the living will worked because she had discussed it with her son, rather than just filling out a form and filing it away. "Living wills are less about control," said Singer, "and more about families facing death together."

But that means people have to talk about death. Unfortunately, spouses and families don't talk about it, mostly because they assume they understand each other so well that they know within a shadow of a doubt whether their loved ones would want to live or die. But in fact, they don't. According to Bowman, research shows that when long-time spouses are put in separate rooms and asked what the other would want, they're right only half the time—as accurate, in other words, as flipping a coin.

When he told me this, I said it sounded like *The Newlywed Game*, a daytime game show that originally ran from 1966 to 1974 and created many rows—and reportedly some divorces—between the contestants. Bowman got a good laugh out of the memory of it. "Oh, that crazy thing," he said before doing a mock wail of a contestant saying, "Oh, I don't *know*!" Then he said, "But these aren't newlyweds; these are long-time partners."

Despite the need for more frank discussion about our wishes, people tend to think, "I don't want to put my wife under a lot of stress, so I'm going to slip off to the lawyer's one afternoon. She'll never have to worry." But then it sits in an envelope somewhere and never finds its way to the ICU anyway. Maybe the family never knows about it, or knows it's in some box at the back of a garage full of junk and isn't up to the prospect of trying to find it or, as happened in one of Bowman's cases, the document is locked in an antique desk that the family deems too valuable to break into.

So living wills only work if there is a conversation that goes with them, because understanding someone's values allows us to understand his or her wishes in any situation. "To simply fill out the form is a bad idea," said Bowman. "You've really got to think about what you want, and you've got to talk to your loved ones about it. If they say they already know, you have to politely say, 'Well, you may not.'" Not that living wills can't help, but the conversation trumps the piece of paper.

8 Nurse Eleanor's Dilemma
One person's struggle with the subject of euthanasia

WHEN KERRY BOWMAN rode the elevator to a consultation one day in the fall of 1999, he had no idea he would soon stumble onto one of the most memorable cases of his career. He was covering Toronto General Hospital at the time and was on his way to meet the family of a patient to talk about how aggressively the medical staff should treat the woman. While his job is rarely routine, a discussion about Do Not Resuscitate status is far from uncommon. Bowman and the family talked by the bed of the unconscious woman, and when they finished, Eleanor, the other patient in the shared room, called him over. She hadn't meant to eavesdrop, she said, but since he was an ethicist, she wondered if she could speak to him about something. He figured she wanted to talk about her doctor or her nurse, but he was off to another meeting, so he promised to come back another time.

True to his word, he returned a couple of days later and pulled up a chair. Bowman had a cup of tea in his hand and Eleanor lay in bed with her tea on a tray. The other bed was empty, so they had some privacy, and the sun streamed into the room. It was a pleasant setting for a long conversation, even if they were in a hospital room.

Gravely ill with liver cancer, Eleanor knew she was close to dying, but she remained lucid. And she was an intelligent and well-read woman. "This situation happened a long time ago," she started with an English accent she'd kept after five decades in Canada, "and I was wondering if I could run it by you." Initially, Bowman assumed she was referring to a few months earlier, or maybe a year, so he was a little surprised to hear that the events had taken place in 1942, when Eleanor was in her early twenties. But he'd had enough experience with old people to know they can quickly end up way back in time. Few had a story like this one, though.

During the Second World War, Eleanor was a British Army nurse stationed at a military hospital in Penang, British Malaya, now known as Malaysia. By January of 1942, amid a swirl of conflicting rumours, Eleanor and her colleagues knew the war was going badly. To avoid being overwhelmed, they tried to concentrate on their work, but the patients couldn't stop talking about it. And as more and more injured arrived in the hospital, everyone realized the Imperial Japanese Army was fast approaching. No one was surprised when the brass ordered an immediate evacuation.

The plan called for doctors, nurses and ambulatory patients to walk eleven miles over difficult terrain to meet British naval ships for transport to Singapore, where they could safely await new orders. But the members of the medical team worried about what to do with the 126 patients who were too severely wounded to walk. The doctors and nurses didn't feel right abandoning their patients, especially since they knew the Japanese preferred bayoneting the injured to capturing them. In addition, word of the evacuation plan—and the imminent attack—had spread quickly among the soldiers, and some of the ones destined to be left behind wanted lethal doses of medication so they could kill themselves rather than be killed or captured by their attackers. A few even asked for hand grenades so they could at least take a few of the enemy with them.

Ignoring his pager, Bowman listened to Eleanor's remarkable story and identified three central ethical questions. The first was about the duty to care. Though "duty to care" wasn't the term Eleanor used, she agreed it was the right one. Terminology aside, the pair knew the problems inherent in trying to apply contemporary bioethics to events that happened not just nearly sixty years earlier, but also during a war. And even today the "duty to care" issue is not a simple one. Some doctors have "fired" patients who refuse to quit smoking, for example, though Bowman is adamant that such a move is unethical. And when some doctors wanted to avoid treating SARS patients during Toronto's two outbreaks in the spring of 2003, Bowman told his bosses at Mount Sinai Hospital that opting out wasn't an option. He believes there may be limits to the duty to care, but ethicists have not sorted out what those limits are—the point at which the medical community could legitimately decide the risks had become too high. "We don't want people committing suicide through their work or anything," Bowman said. "But there definitely is a duty to care— we're still trying to untangle it."

Like the other doctors and nurses in the military hospital, Eleanor felt she had an absolute responsibility to take care of her patients. But she also knew what awaited her if she stayed: incarceration in a prisoner of war camp under horrible conditions was about the best she could hope for. She'd heard about the beatings, the rapes and the killing of patients in front of their nurses that took place in the camps after the fall of Shanghai and Hong Kong. Also, malaria and dysentery were rampant, and the Japanese, who didn't adhere to the Geneva Conventions, often refused to give their prisoners access to Red Cross supplies.

The second issue—and to both Eleanor and Bowman the most difficult—concerned assisted suicide and euthanasia. The soldiers who couldn't leave were begging for a way to kill themselves when the Japanese arrived. Eleanor believed their requests were based on dignity rather than fear; they just didn't want to die by a Japanese sword. Worse, some patients were so badly burned that someone else would need to put the fatal doses of drugs in their mouths rather than just in their hands. And that would mean even more active involvement in the "mercy killing"—though ethically, Bowman didn't think there was much difference.

Finally, the medical team had to decide whether to give the bed-ridden soldiers the weapons they wanted. Added to the ethical dilemma of doctors and nurses becoming active participants in the war was the issue that exploding hand grenades might incite the Japanese to become even more brutal and turn their machine guns on the whole place, killing everyone.

With just eleven or twelve hours to go before everyone had to be down at the shore eleven miles away, they didn't have a lot of time to debate the finer points of medical ethics. There was no need, everyone agreed, for all four doctors and eight nurses to stay behind; besides, they knew they would be needed elsewhere. If the war was going so badly, it didn't make sense to have a lot of medical personnel stuck in camps. So they decided that one doctor and one nurse would remain behind. And to determine who stayed and who went, they drew straws.

Before they did, they agreed that any member of the team could drop out of the lottery at any time without explanation. No one did. Eleanor wasn't surprised: she figured everyone else was as frightened as she was, but there really wasn't any alternative. They certainly couldn't leave wounded men to fend for themselves in tropical conditions with an army advancing. Though terrifying, that decision was straightforward. And refusing to give patients hand grenades was the only real choice.

But the medical team still had to deal with the requests for drugs from the remaining soldiers.

This was what haunted Eleanor the most as she lay in bed telling her story to Bowman. It was killing, she knew—but under those conditions, was it okay? Could there be one form of moral reasoning for wartime and another for peacetime? And if there could, should there be? What does it say about the human condition if we can hold different standards in war than in peace? She believed that people should live with integrity no matter what the situation.

Bowman didn't ask her what, in the end, she'd personally concluded that day in 1942; she just said that after much debate they'd reached a consensus and handed the drugs to the desperate men. Then Eleanor and the others who had drawn long straws left for Singapore, but before long the port was under such heavy bombardment that all European women and children had to evacuate. Although they questioned the wisdom of an order that removed the nurses, Eleanor and her friends sailed under the cover of night with the understanding that if they made it ten hours from shore they'd be out of range of the Japanese bombers. But eleven hours out, they suddenly heard war planes overhead. A lot of people died in the attack, the ship sank and Eleanor found herself in the water in a life jacket. Along with others, she floated to Sumatra and ended up in a prisoner of war camp in Aceh—where she was reunited with the nurse who had pulled the short straw.

In early 1946, after she'd been liberated and had regained her health, Eleanor tried to tell her superiors. But they didn't want to hear it. Their attitude was they didn't owe anyone an explanation for what happened under those conditions, so they patted her on the head and told her never to speak of it again. Orders aside, because she was one of the few survivors, she had no one to talk to about what had happened at that military hospital. In fact, until her conversation with Bowman, she hadn't really spoken about her war experience at all. For a long time she didn't really want to discuss it, and when she did, people quickly grew uncomfortable because they weren't in those camps and the stories are so horrible. "You just don't go for tea with sixty-year-old women and talk about what it was like in a Japanese prisoner of war camp," she said. "People just don't want to hear it."

And that's why, after living so long with so much guilt, and about to die, she turned to a hospital ethicist. On one level, she just wanted someone who would listen, but she was also looking for some kind of absolution, and since she wasn't religious, a chaplain wouldn't do. An ethicist was perfect. He explained that just because he had a Ph.D. in ethics didn't mean he had all the answers or was even able to say what was right and what was wrong. "I don't know what I would have said or done," Bowman told her, "but you did the best you possibly could do under those conditions."

They discussed her case at length. And Bowman was able to be honest with her and give her some of the understanding she sought. "I am not horrendously anti-euthanasia to begin with," he admitted later. "My main concern with euthanasia is the slippery slope. We're not good at caring for the dying in Canada—or virtually anywhere else. If we're to suddenly have euthanasia tomorrow, we might have people saying they'd rather be dead because we can't provide pain control and support. So my position is, let's improve the care of the dying before we can really shine a true ethical light on euthanasia. This case was very different than that."

Bowman believed he gave Eleanor huge comfort. He didn't think she did anything morally abhorrent and he told her so. "Yeah, part of that was trying to appease her, but I wasn't lying," he said. "Probably if I were in her situation, I would have done the same thing, but I wasn't in her situation, so I don't know."

After talking with Eleanor for more than ninety minutes, he was late for his next meeting, so he had to go. But he returned to her bedside several times, visiting even after she lost consciousness. She died three weeks after she'd first told him her story, and her death touched him even more than most. "I felt horrible when she died," he admitted. "I had a lot of respect for her."

9 An Emergency Exit
The case for euthanasia and assisted suicide

ROBERT BUCKMAN doesn't mind admitting that he once gave a patient a lethal injection. Back in 1978, he was a medical resident in his native England, and his patient, a German woman of about sixty years of age, had suffered an aneurysm that released a huge amount of blood into her central nervous system. Initially she stabilized, and to a certain extent recovered; in fact, she was walking and talking and the neurosurgeon planned to operate. Before he had a chance, though, the woman suffered a second bleed about eight days later that left her unconscious with no cerebral function. But she was not on a ventilator.

The patient's husband, a man in his mid-sixties, took it hard. Over the next two or three weeks, he deteriorated dramatically. The formerly rotund man started losing so much weight that a huge gap developed between his shirt collar and his neck. He stopped shaving and he looked a wreck. He finally admitted that he wished his wife would die.

The staff physician, the head nurse, the intern and Buckman met for an informal meeting and everyone agreed that it would be a kindness for this woman to die. As the resident, Buckman won the job of injecting her with potassium chloride. While his actions were, strictly speaking, illegal, they were also accepted practice in English hospitals at the time. And he soon understood why. "Her death restored her husband," he told the audience of a seminar I attended at the Joint Centre for Bioethics. "I don't regret it. I still think I—we—did the right thing."

Today, he proposes that if someone with a terminal illness and only a few months to live makes repeated, coherent requests to die, a doctor should be able to fill out a detailed form and send it off to the Crown attorney's office, which would then send someone to interview the patient. Upon approval of the request, the doctor would have two to three weeks to perform euthanasia. After the first hundred cases, the government could analyze all of them and publish the results. He considers it "a very Canadian way of dealing with this." (And no doubt he'd find agreement from both those who favour regulation and fairness and those who think "Canadian" is a euphemism for "bureaucratic.")

Buckman figures few people would actually opt for it. Comparing it to the life vests under the seats on airplanes—seldom if ever used, but a comfort just by their existence—he said, "It would be an emergency exit that most people would feel glad was there. But the vast majority of people, in my opinion, would not use it. I think we'd be talking about dozens of cases per year."

ALTHOUGH "EUTHANASIA" (from the Greek) means "good death," it also means one hell of a controversial subject. Even the word is contentious, and not just because of the baggage it carries from Nazi Germany. Activists on both sides of the issue want to frame the debate, and part of the strategy is to own the terminology. (Anti-abortionists, for example, successfully convinced the media and the public to use "pro-life," a meaningless term—who is *against* life?—yet powerful branding.) Those fighting the adoption of anything like Buckman's proposal favour the word "euthanasia," so it's no coincidence that Alex Schadenberg, one of Canada's leading opponents of any liberalization of the law, is the executive director of a group called the Euthanasia Prevention Coalition. Advocates on the other side—sometimes called the right-to-die movement—haven't been able to agree on a suitably unthreatening word or phrase, but prefer terms such as "assisted dying," "hastening dying" and "dying with dignity." (Both sides like that last word: one of the Euthanasia Prevention Coalition's objectives is to increase the "understanding and respect for the dignity of human life.")

Personally, I'm going with the only source that really matters: the *Canadian Oxford Dictionary* defines euthanasia as "an act of painlessly killing, esp. at the patient's request, a person or animal suffering from an incurable condition." Besides, this is an issue where winning the nomenclature battle hasn't made much of a difference. While those in the medical community may shy away from the term, most people in the general public aren't afraid of the word and in fact throw it around rather loosely, using "euthanasia" to cover everything from withdrawing or withholding treatment to assisted suicide to mercy killing. But there are important distinctions between the acts.

Withdrawing or withholding treatment—occasionally referred to as "passive euthanasia," though that phrase has fallen out of favour—is neither illegal nor considered unethical in Canada. A doctor may remove or refuse to offer treatments, including ventilators, drugs and feeding tubes, if that's what the patient wants (and if the patient is unable to communicate, the doctor should turn to the family for guidance). It's true that some people find this practice deeply offensive, especially when it involves a feeding tube, as we all discovered during the Terri Schiavo saga. "Withdrawing tube-feeding from a person is one of the most emotionally sensitive issues that I ever have dealt with in my career in clinical bioethics," Sue MacRae told me when she was the deputy director of the JCB. "Any family member who is faced with that decision is ripped up about it. There is something about food and water that is utterly human for people." Nevertheless, every day, in hospitals across the country, doctors remove feeding tubes and other life-sustaining treatments.

While intentionally killing a patient with drugs is illegal, the so-called double effect is acceptable. When, for example, a doctor administers morphine to ease the patient's suffering, the drug may have two effects: one positive (the relief of pain) and one negative (a hastened death). As long as the doctor's intention was to ease the pain, not kill the patient, he or she has done nothing illegal or unethical. It's maybe a too-convenient bit of reasoning: a doctor who gives a patient drugs because she's in pain is a virtuous person, while one who prescribes the same dose because the patient is going to die anyway and the doctor believes hastening the inevitable is the right thing to do, is a murderer. But intent is hard to prove or disprove and nobody is going to admit to homicide, so a "don't ask, don't tell" policy reigns. Sometimes doctors do face furious family members accusing them of drugging a loved one to death—or "snowing her until death"—though many other families know exactly what's going on and believe it's for the best.

"Assisted suicide" is the provision of drugs or other means that a person will use to take his or her own life. When a doctor is the provider, we call it "doctor-assisted suicide." One of the most famous cases of doctor-assisted suicide in Canada is that of Sue Rodriguez. In 1992, the Victoria, B.C., woman learned at age forty-two that she had ALS. A neurological disorder, amyotrophic lateral sclerosis—or Lou Gehrig's Disease—attacks the nerve cells that control muscles. The patient's mind, personality, intelligence, memory and senses, however, remain unaffected. Most people with ALS die of respiratory failure within three to five years, though some can live for a decade or more. Rodriguez challenged the law against assisted suicide. After the Supreme Court decided five to four against her, she defied the ruling and with an anonymous doctor as well as New Democratic Party MP Svend Robinson present, died in February 1994. Despite all the publicity the case generated, police laid no charges.

The "euthanasia" Buckman advocates legalizing—and what some people consider "voluntary euthanasia"—would allow a doctor to administer a lethal dose of drugs to a patient who is dying but conscious and competent, and asks for it, but only after the government has approved the request. Other advocates go further and want to see doctors allowed to perform the same act if a living will calls for it.

The taking of another person's life for compassionate reasons without his or her permission is sometimes called a "mercy killing," though that's another phrase often used imprecisely. An example of this type of "non-voluntary euthanasia" was the Robert Latimer case. Latimer was the Saskatchewan farmer who decided he had no choice but to end the painful life of Tracy, his twelve-year-old daughter who was born with severe cerebral palsy. A quadriplegic who weighed just forty pounds, Tracy had suffered through many surgeries and was scheduled to have her thighbone removed. In 1993, her father put her in the cab of his Chevy pickup and, with a hose from the exhaust pipe, pumped in carbon monoxide.

The story was tragic and the ensuing legal battle tortuous. Charged with first-degree murder, Latimer was convicted of second-degree murder and received the mandatory minimum life sentence with no chance of full parole for ten years. He appealed to the Supreme Court of Canada on the grounds that the prosecution had tampered with the jury by getting the

RCMP to question potential jurors about their views on euthanasia and abortion. After winning his appeal, he faced a second trial for second-degree murder and was again convicted. This time, the judge ignored the mandatory minimum—ruling that under the circumstances it would be cruel and unusual punishment—and sentenced Latimer to two years less a day, with one year in prison and one under house arrest. When he appealed his conviction and the Crown appealed the sentence, the Saskatchewan Court of Appeal gave him the mandatory minimum. The Supreme Court upheld that ruling. He began serving his sentence in 2001 and applied for day parole in 2007. He seemed like the perfect candidate for it since he'd been a model prisoner and wasn't a risk to reoffend, but the parole board denied his application because he wouldn't say killing his daughter had been a mistake. A review board later reversed this decision and he started day parole in 2008.

Latimer's fate divided Canadians into two steadfastly opposed groups. On one side, many people—almost three-quarters of the country, according to one poll—believed the sentence was far too harsh for what Latimer saw as an act of compassion, however wrong-headed it might have been. Others, particularly advocates for the disabled, saw the case as one of murder, pure and simple. On top of that, the various twists and turns of Latimer's legal battle suggested that the charges and the sentencing in such cases might have less to do with the law and more to do with the religious and moral beliefs of prosecutors and the judges.

What Latimer did was so blatant that some charges were inevitable, but it's not hard to imagine that another province might have charged him with a lesser offence. Jocelyn Downie is an ethicist who comes from a law background. In her book, *Dying Justice: A Case for Decriminalizing Euthanasia and Assisted*

Suicide in Canada, Downie, the director of the Health Law Institute at Halifax's Dalhousie University, explains that one reason we need to reform our euthanasia laws is that courts in different provinces treat these cases differently. A health care worker in Nova Scotia might be charged with murder, for example, while one in Ontario who'd done the same thing might be allowed to plead guilty to administering a noxious substance. Even within provinces there are variations, because Crown attorneys all have their own views on the subject.

Downie also argues that there's an inconsistency between the Criminal Code and the actual administration of justice, because the code says euthanasia is murder, but it's usually treated as a less serious crime. She's not against prosecutorial discretion, just against "a situation in which prosecutorial discretion is taken to an extreme."

Her third reason is that "we are failing the dying, along with their families, friends, and health care providers." Her evidence here includes the fact that patients die in pain; that some patients try to commit suicide and end up worse off when they fail; that patients can be forced to stay alive even if "they think that life is no longer worth living"; that people who try to help patients or loved ones can end up facing life imprisonment with no chance for parole for twenty-five years; that people may commit suicide "earlier than they would if assisted suicide were legal because they fear getting to that point when they need, but would not have access to, assisted suicide"; and that people are turning to the likes of Jack Kevorkian, the American doctor who helped more than one hundred people die between 1990 and 1998.

SURVEYS CONSISTENTLY SHOW that the majority of Canadians don't have a big problem with assisted suicide. According to an Ipsos Reid poll in 2007, for example, 71 percent of us believe that doctors should be allowed to assist in the death of terminally ill patients. Still, Buckman was hardly preaching to the converted when he spoke to those attending the seminar at the JCB. He talked for about thirty-five minutes and then opened the floor to questions. Most of them were polite but gently challenging. When it was over, Kerry Bowman—who knew many people in the audience, of course, and was sure there was a strong bias against euthanasia in the room—told me he was surprised at the diplomatic reception Buckman received.

Despite the views of the general public, most people who work in health care don't want to see euthanasia legalized. That may be because the people embedded in the complexity of health care and ethics understand how teams make decisions and how policies can get misconstrued. In other words, they know how imperfect the system is. True, most health care professionals and bioethicists—everyone but the most vociferous critics of euthanasia—can imagine a situation that would lead them to say, "Yes, people should be allowed to kill themselves." But the fear is that it's a big leap between the principle and a workable policy that would make it possible.

People who work in palliative care tend to be those most offended by the prospect of legal euthanasia. They often believe a patient who wants to die is suffering a spiritual crisis and really just needs love and support. But for Bowman, "There's nothing more horrible than mandatory intimacy. It's, 'You've got this crisis, you want to be dead, I'm now your best friend and I want to explore your soul.' Yuck!" He stretched out the last word for emphasis. That's fine for those who really want it, but some people don't want to explore their soul with a stranger. They really want to be dead.

We will die the way we lived; and since we all live differently, we will die differently too. So Bowman was open to Buckman's argument and thought he'd made some good points in the seminar. But the ethicist did think the doctor had made a mistake by opening his talk with the case of the German woman. "I think what he wanted to say was, 'I want to break this taboo. I want to tell you I've done this and I don't regret this.'" But it wasn't a good example, because the medical team didn't really know whether the patient wanted to die or not.

After we'd talked for over an hour in Bowman's office, we decided to decamp to the Roof Lounge at the Park Hyatt Hotel. We talked about his ape work for a bit and then we got around to the big subject: "People hate it when I say this," he declared, "but I'm not convinced there's a huge moral difference between killing and letting die."

I mentioned Schiavo yet again. A doctor could have given her an injection rather than let her starve to death over thirteen days. Wouldn't that have been better for everybody?

"Well, the medical people would say that what you're talking about in the first case is cold-blooded murder and in the second it's nature taking its course, and they're radically different."

He elaborated by presenting me with "the same old corny, stupid case": a man walking his dog down by the water sees that his cousin, from whom he will inherit three million dollars, has fallen off a pier into Lake Ontario and is flailing about in the water. If the man and his dog just keep walking and let him drown, is that morally any different from holding the cousin's head under until he's dead? One is letting die and one is killing. Legally, there's a huge difference in the two scenarios, but law and ethics are not the same. "We all hang our hats on the fact that there's a massive distinction," said Bowman, who noted that he had changed his perspective after years of working with dying patients. "Mind you, I'll say smugly that most of us have never thought too deeply about whether those two things are different or not. But we assume they are. Radically different—not slightly different, radically different."

And yet Bowman has two serious objections to euthanasia. The first is the potential devaluing of the lives of disabled people. If we say euthanasia is legal, the danger is we are saying some forms of life may not be worth living. I pointed out that Buckman argued that only terminal patients would be eligible and no one else could make the decision for them—in other words, to use the medical jargon, there'd be no "substitute decision making." But such a provision might not withstand a legal challenge because doctors regularly rely on families in end-of-life cases, as so often the patient is not competent or not conscious. Someone is going to argue, "My father said he wanted to die this morning, just before he lapsed into the coma. He was just about to call the doctor when he keeled over."

Bowman's second concern is that if the quality of the care is poor, people will ask for euthanasia because they are in unnecessary pain, not because they really want to die. "I think if we have a single Canadian who is asking for euthanasia because we're not providing the kind of end-of-life care we should be providing— that we're capable of providing them with—then it's a moral problem."

It's also a medical and legal problem. Even most religious groups accept the double-effect concept, but not all doctors understand that if their goal is pain control and comfort, they can medicate to whatever point is necessary without fear of prosecution. When it comes to dying, what people are most afraid of is pain, and yet they often go undermedicated because doctors fear they'll be thrown in jail for killing their patients. "It's a Catch-22," said MacRae. "Doctors aren't adequately managing their patients' pain because they're afraid of the legal implications of euthanasia. But as a result of not adequately taking care of the pain, the public wants euthanasia because they're afraid of being in pain."

Those two—not inconsiderable—hurdles aside, Bowman isn't against euthanasia, though he would never perform it, because it's illegal and he has no interest in going to prison. "I really do see a lot of reasons for euthanasia, but I can't get past those two concerns," he said. "But euthanasia itself doesn't particularly offend me."

AFTER BUCKMAN'S LECTURE, I waited to introduce myself to him. He warned me off shaking his hand because he had a cold, but agreed to meet with me a few weeks later. In the meantime, I took the opportunity to read his autobiography. Despite its title—*Not Dead Yet: The Unauthorized Biography of Dr. Robert Buckman*—the entertaining book doesn't deal with euthanasia. Instead, it tells the story of how he started out in medicine as "a little prick with a needle" and managed to be both a doctor and a comic actor and writer. In 1985, he moved to Canada, where he continued to work as an oncologist but also increasingly used his strong communication skills. His *What You Really Need to Know about* ... series of videos on various diseases, created with the help of Monty Python's John Cleese, generated a series of books with the same name. He's also done a lot of television, including hosting a medical show on TVOntario

For several years, Buckman also taught at the University of Toronto's Faculty of Medicine. In his course, called Ethics and Communication, he argued that communication skills could often eliminate ethical problems. He cited the example of the doctor who is convinced his cancer patient will commit suicide if he finds out he's dying. Should the doctor tell the patient the truth? Buckman's answer is simple: communicate differently. If the doctor can talk to the patient, support him, explain about palliative care, find out what he's most afraid of, and deal with those fears, then maybe suicide won't seem like the only option.

A plate of orange wedges and a Starbucks coffee cup sat on his desk as he told me about how in the 1970s he almost ended up in a fistfight with a chaplaincy student who had suggested that suffering brings out our humanity. "Bullshit," Buckman told him. "You have no idea." The student had never seen anybody suffering in severe, uncontrolled pain. "Come and look at a person on the second day of a dental abscess and look at the humanity—it's out the window. The one thing all patients suffering severe pain lose is their individuality and humanity."

Nevertheless, Buckman hadn't taken any particular interest in euthanasia as a public policy issue when he lived in England. But after he moved to Canada, Dying with Dignity—an organization dedicated to improving "the quality of dying for all Canadians in accordance with their own wishes, values, and beliefs"—approached him. Believing that "a legal, peaceable, decent campaign to change the law" was a good idea, he said, "Oh, well, sure."

Because he hadn't covered them in his lecture, I ran Bowman's doubts about euthanasia by him. But Buckman wasn't concerned about devaluing the lives of disabled people, because under his proposal the approval process would prevent abuse and he insisted that the government should prosecute anyone who performed unauthorized euthanasia. Nor was he buying the suggestion that poor health care would prompt people to ask to be killed. Although he admitted that the idea of offering palliative care before approving euthanasia was a good one, he pointed out that since he'd arrived in Canada, only three of his patients have asked him about euthanasia. In each case, he insisted, it didn't have anything to do with the quality of the care. They simply didn't want to go through what awaited them for any longer than they had to. But, of course, if asking to die were a legal option, more patients would raise the subject.

Buckman didn't think the audience at the JCB seminar was skeptical. In fact, he wasn't even sure that the majority of health care workers *are* against euthanasia. "If it is most, it's so even, it's so like fifty-fifty that if the law changed and it was abuse-free— if the protections against abuse were there—I don't think they'd have any problem at all," he said, noting that instead of feeling any backlash from colleagues, he's experienced the exact opposite. "But isn't that the way humans are? People come up to you and say, 'I so agree with you.' So to me, it feels like 99.3 percent of people are in favour of it because the people I meet are the ones who say, 'That needed to be said.'"

Either way, if Canada adopted Buckman's proposal, doctors who were against euthanasia would never be forced to perform it. And those who did would be unlikely to be harassed, attacked and even killed the way doctors who offer abortions have been. With around one hundred thousand abortions in Canada every year and busy, easy-to-find clinics, doctors who perform them are ready targets, but Buckman figured that approved requests for euthanasia would be rare; the average doctor might do it once or twice in his or her career and many never would. Indeed, doctor-assisted suicide became legal in Oregon in 1997, but by 2008, only 341 people had taken advantage of it.

He also believes that any euthanasia law must ensure that doctors perform it only when a competent patient requests it. That means it wouldn't have made any difference in a case like Schiavo's. ("Tough luck," he said. "Because that is a very, very slippery slope.") Nor would it have applied in the Robert Latimer case. While Buckman believes Latimer was well meaning, he's adamant that only doctors should perform euthanasia. "We can't countenance non-physicians doing what he did," he said. "We're a case like that permitted by law, I think that would open a huge floodgate for anybody murdering anybody at any time and saying, 'Well, actually, I did shoot Derek in the brain, but Derek hasn't been feeling too well lately and asked me to kill him.' And I think that's wrong."

Still, he doesn't think Latimer's punishment fit the crime and admitted he had thought that when the publicity waned the sentence would be reduced. "But I think they were probably afraid—and not unreasonably—that the brouhaha would light up immediately the moment he walked out. It might be easier to change the law."

Of course, changing the law is no easy matter. "I guess there are two reasons against it. One is huge, which is the potential for abuse," he said. "The other, which is equally huge, is that some people think it's taking away something that God has given—as if God created pneumonia and God created antibiotics and God ordered the physicians to give the antibiotics but not to withdraw them."

Buckman is president of the Humanist Association of Canada and author of *Can We Be Good Without God? An Exploration of Behaviour, Belonging and the Need to Believe.* I didn't have a problem with that because I'm also an atheist. To me, that fact is no more remarkable than, say, that I have blue eyes. But I've discovered that admitting atheism to other people may be incautious. A few years after the death of my father, who had been a Presbyterian elder, I met a woman who had been his friend.

"There's nothing like a continuing Presbyterian," she said fondly of him.

"Yeah, well," I said matter-of-factly, "I'm an atheist."

"Oh, don't say 'atheist,' dear. Say 'agnostic.'"

That was many years ago, but my atheism still seems to surprise people, even those who aren't churchgoers. Now that I was sitting in Buckman's office, I wanted to know what role his atheism played in his pro-euthanasia stance. So I started to ask, "You're an evangelical atheist—"

"I think that's a very nice way of putting it," he jumped in. Then he thought about it for a second. "Evangelical ... I would say I'm a mildly proselytizing atheist. 'Evangelical' I'm a little worried about, because it means different things to different people. But I like to tell people, if they ask, that I'm an atheist, only because the general public are still a little bit wary and think that if you're an atheist you've got to be an immoral, lying, cheating bastard who'll do something horrible to their daughters. I don't think I'm particularly wonderfully virtuous or anything, but I think I'm a fairly normal guy. And I like it to be acknowledged that you can be a normal, decent guy and not believe all the rules and regulations came down on a set of tablets."

I then finished my question: "Is there any connection between your atheism and your attitude toward euthanasia?"

"None at all," he said. But when I asked him what he'd learned from years of speaking out on the issue, he couldn't help but comment on the hypocrisy of some people whose religious beliefs dictate their stance on euthanasia. "One of the things that surprised me is that several of the people who object to the idea of euthanasia have very strongly held views that God—a god— is controlling everything and that we'd best leave it to him, and they don't see any inconsistency with what they do every day. Even intensive care nurses who are saving lives left, right and centre—they're intervening against 'God's will' and yet say that euthanasia is somehow playing God."

During Buckman's seminar at the JCB, when he told the story of performing euthanasia back in London, he admitted that he didn't know if he'd have given the woman the injection if it meant losing his licence and going to jail. He repeated that position in his office when he told me about one of the three patients who'd asked him about euthanasia. She was a young woman with breast cancer. The cancer had spread widely into the bone, and they did discuss euthanasia at length. He told her he couldn't do it because he didn't want to go to prison, but he could offer palliative sedation to maintain her in a coma. The next day, though, she fell into a coma on her own and died ten days later.

Buckman is an articulate and entertaining advocate for the legalization of euthanasia and says, "If you think the law is wrong, you change the law; you don't just do what you think is right." But that kind of change won't happen without champions willing to make greater sacrifices. For years, many Canadians believed in a woman's right to an abortion, but we needed Henry Morgentaler, a stubborn crusader, to change the law. He performed illegal abortions, went to jail and fought his case all the way to the Supreme Court of Canada, while suffering not just public criticism but organized protests; his opponents even bombed his Toronto clinic and attacked him with garden shears. It was a battle that took over twenty years and enormous courage.

The problem for euthanasia advocates in Canada is that Buckman is rare among doctors and ethicists for his willingness even to speak publicly on the subject. Kerry Bowman, who is happy to call for a debate on the subject but won't be an activist for legalization, believes that euthanasia, like abortion, is a taboo subject for many. "We ethicists rarely talk about it," he told me. "It's taught that it's completely and utterly wrong and it's not open for discussion."

Back when those who contracted AIDS regularly died from the disease, most people in the gay community knew family doctors who were willing to risk helping patients die. They just didn't publicize it. One doctor, Maurice Genereux, did plead guilty in 1997 to prescribing fatal doses of drugs to two HIV-positive men and became the first doctor to be convicted of assisted suicide in Canada. But there was more to this unusual case. For one thing, Genereux had previously been charged with sexual offences involving his patients. For another, the partner of the man who committed suicide (the other one only attempted it) wrote about it in a newspaper, and the publicity may have prompted the charges.

Mostly, though, doctors and ethicists have been unwilling to be champions for assisted suicide and euthanasia. And that means it's been left to ordinary citizens to push for change.

One of those ordinary citizens was Evelyn Martens. In 2004, the seventy-three-year-old executive director of the Right to Die Network of Canada was acquitted of two counts of aiding and abetting suicide, which carries a maximum penalty of fourteen years. Martens had become active in the push for legalizing euthanasia after her brother died a painful death from cancer. She began selling "exit bags," which feature Velcro collars that allow a tight fit so that helium can be pumped into the plastic bag through a hose, resulting in death in a few seconds. She had requests for them from people all over the world

Early in 2002, Martens was present when Monique Charest, a former nun who lived in Duncan, B.C., killed herself using an exit bag. Six months later, police followed Martens to the Vancouver home of Leyanne Burchell, a teacher with stomach cancer. Later that day, when Martens stepped off the ferry on Vancouver Island, police arrested her and found exit bags, helium tanks and sleep-inducing drugs in her van and home.

Other examples, however, seem more like exceptions than good test cases. Mary Fogarty, for instance, was convicted in 1995 of giving her diabetic friend, Brenda Barnes, syringes and insulin and writing her suicide note. Fogarty claimed that Barnes had dictated the note to her and that she hadn't realized what it was. And while she admitted to giving her friend syringes, she suggested that Barnes had taken the insulin from Fogarty's purse. Meanwhile, the Crown contended that Fogarty mistakenly thought she would benefit from a one-hundred-thousand-dollar life insurance policy. The judge sentenced her to three years probation and three hundred hours of community service, making her the first person in over thirty years to be convicted of assisted suicide in Canada. In *Dying Justice*, Jocelyn Downie points out that this is an unusual case, because "the jury concluded that Fogarty assisted her friend to commit suicide out of self-interest rather than out of a desire to help a competent friend end a life of unrelenting suffering."

Also murky, though in a different way, is the case of Marielle Houle, a Montreal nursing home employee who helped her son, Charles Fariala, commit suicide in 2004. Diagnosed with multiple sclerosis a year earlier, the thirty-six-year-old playwright had trouble walking but was otherwise in reasonably good shape. Still, he told friends he wanted to die before the disease progressed too far. Police charged Houle with aiding and abetting a suicide. While her arrest attracted some media attention, right-to-die activists weren't especially eager to embrace her cause. Since Fariala's condition was not unbearable and his death wasn't imminent—and because he may have been suffering from depression—he wouldn't have met the criteria for assisted suicide under the kind of legislation most people would like to see. In addition, Houle was not out to change the law—only to help her son. Her lawyer, Salvatore Mascia, told the *National Post*, "She doesn't want to be a martyr."

Marcel Tremblay wasn't afraid to be a martyr. When he announced his plans to kill himself in 2005, he definitely meant it as a political statement. The seventy-eight-year-old Ottawa man suffered from idiopathic pulmonary fibrosis, a lung disease that would eventually kill him. He was also a supporter of Dying with Dignity and he wanted to see a debate on assisted suicide. So on a frigid Friday night at the end of January, a few days after he'd made his announcement, he attended his own wake with about fifty friends and family members at a restaurant in Kanata's Holiday Inn Select. He ate two shrimp and a crab cake and drank a couple of beers. Then he went back to his bungalow and, surrounded by his family, used a plastic turkey-basting bag, a hose and a rented tank of helium to kill himself.

Although his family was with him, he didn't need anyone's help to die, so it wasn't really a case of assisted suicide and the police laid no charges. And while his act certainly generated media coverage—Tremblay appeared on *Canada AM* on the day of his wake, and that night a throng of reporters gathered outside his home—it was a typical media blip: a story for a couple of days and then quickly forgotten. Headlines such as "Suicide Sparks Emotional Debate," which appeared above a *Toronto Star* story, were common, as were stories that canvassed the opinions of public-issue ethicists. Nevertheless, precious few Canadians talked about Tremblay at cocktail parties or in local bars or around the dining room table, so his dreams of igniting a debate or thoughtful deliberation proved futile.

In most of the world, euthanasia remains illegal, but some countries are at least holding the debate. In 2008, Luxembourg's parliament approved assisted suicide and euthanasia—and then reduced the monarch's powers when Grand Duke Henri refused to give the legislation royal assent. The Netherlands officially legalized assisted suicide and euthanasia in 2002, though the practice had been unofficially accepted since 1984. The new legislation stipulated that the patient must ask to die, be suffering badly and have no chance of recovering. In addition, a second doctor has to approve the decision. In Belgium, which also legalized euthanasia in 2002, a psychologist must agree with the two doctors if there are any doubts about the competency of the patient. The country also insists that patients go through a palliative care consultation. Many people change their minds after learning more about their options. Switzerland forbids euthanasia, but assisted suicide—even if it doesn't involve a doctor—has been legal there since 1941.

The first North American jurisdiction to allow doctor-assisted suicide is Oregon. After voters approved the idea in 1994, the legislation survived a legal challenge and became law in 1997. It covers adults with a terminal illness and no more than six months to live, as long as the person concerned is not suffering from depression that would cause impaired judgment or from some other mental disorder. The appeal must persist for fifteen days and then be verified by two doctors and two witnesses who aren't family members or primary caregivers. Additional safeguards include ensuring that the patient is aware of pain management and palliative care options. In November of 2008, the residents of Washington State voted for a similar measure by a margin of 59 percent to 41 percent.

The Special Senate Committee on Euthanasia and Assisted Suicide, which Buckman appeared before, released its final report in 1995, recommending no changes to Canadian law. Late in 2004, in the aftermath of all the publicity surrounding the cases of Evelyn Martens, Marielle Houle and others, then justice minister Irwin Cotler told the House of Commons justice committee that it was time to reopen the debate. Of course, saying it and doing it are entirely different things, especially for a cabinet minister in a precarious minority government. Rather than wait for Cotler, Bloc Québécois MP Francine Lalonde introduced a private member's bill on assisted suicide in 2005. It died with the non-confidence vote that brought down the Liberal government, but it wasn't likely to go anywhere anyway, and not just because private members' bills rarely pass. As soon as a controversial ethical issue such as euthanasia comes up, too many of our politicians scatter like cockroaches confronted by a kitchen light.

Bowman, for one, doesn't think we'll see legal euthanasia in Canada in his lifetime because the public is too divided and the medical community is too strongly against it. Buckman is more optimistic. "In my gut, I sort of feel that it probably will change, probably within a decade. And I would like to see it change in an incredibly circumscribed set of circumstances with incredible scrutiny so there's absolutely none of the 'Oh, she's not doing so well, let's give her a shot.' I think it's extremely important to do it right."

Was he confident it would be done right?

"Yes, this is Canada," said Buckman, who has lived in this country for more than two decades. "I mean that very sincerely."

10 Leaving Home
A journey in search
of a dignified death

IN 2007, ERIC MACDONALD, a sixty-five-year-old recently retired Anglican priest, accompanied his thirty-eight-year-old wife, Elizabeth, who was suffering from advanced multiple sclerosis, as she travelled from their home in Windsor, Nova Scotia, to Zurich, Switzerland. There, she took advantage of that country's liberalized assisted suicide laws and the expertise of Dignitas, an organization that helps people die with dignity. Here, in Eric's own words, is their story.

Elizabeth's first symptom was on September 6, 1998, and by mid-October we had a pretty good idea what it was. She had an appointment with a neurologist in November, and she said, "I think I have MS." The neurologist said, "Well, we'd never give you a diagnosis before you've had an MRI." But later, he looked at her and said, "I've never told a patient this before, but I think you've got MS, too." She had her MRI in December and that was confirmed in January.

When she got her diagnosis, she said, "Well, I guess I should think about selling my business." She had a small printing business. And the doctor said, "There's no reason you should do that. There are lots of people with MS who live many, many years, and we'll get you on Interferon quickly and we should be able to slow the disease down." But nothing, absolutely nothing, retarded the progress of the disease.

In January 2002, we went to the Ottawa General Hospital, because they were running a research program on bone marrow transplants. It was a very risky thing. The idea was to destroy the immune system and then reboot it, in a sense, by bone marrow transplant. But her disease had progressed so quickly and so far that the risk committee would not accept her into the program. Coming out of the hospital, she turned to me and said, "You know, that's a sentence of death."

And, really, it was. That was the crucial moment, because she felt that we'd tried everything and nothing had worked. We had plenty of opportunities to talk about it, because there were times when things got too much for her. And for me too. She would have what she called a meltdown, and we would talk about things for a while and I would try to encourage her from time to time. I knew that things weren't going well.

Elizabeth had a lot of pain. By January of 1999, when the doctor said, "On a scale of one to ten, where would you put your pain?" she said, "Hmmm, twelve?" She also said, "It feels as though the bone in my leg is splintering and I look down and wonder why there aren't bones sticking out through the skin."`

Sometimes during the night she would cry out in pain, because when she was lying down her legs would go into spasm. A spasm in the legs is just like having a charley horse, and you know what that pain is like. I used to have to get up and straighten out her legs to relieve some of the spasticity and then turn her so that she could get some relief. So during the night, sometimes she would cry out in pain. But on other occasions she was a remarkably cheerful person. She never let on that she was in pain and she never allowed other people, certainly outside the house, to see her in pain. Nobody ever saw that.

I would try my best to encourage her to go one more mile. But she kept a journal during this period, and sometimes she would write that she was not quite sure I was aware of how much distress she was really in.

But the worst part wasn't the pain. It was the impending loss of control, the impending complete paralysis. The sense of being completely helpless, the inability to move or even to speak. Elizabeth knew one person who couldn't speak and was completely paralyzed, and she had no intention of following in those footsteps. From her point of view, his quality of life was very poor. They were fairly wealthy so they could afford full-time nursing care at home. But she was decided, at that point, that she was certainly not going to stay around for that. That was a quality of life she was not willing to endure. Her grandfather had had MS too, and died not completely paralyzed but almost paralyzed. She could remember, from when she was a young girl, how terrible his situation seemed to her.

It was coming, she knew that. Her arms and hands were numb and were becoming more and more numb. Her face was numb. Her voice was starting to suffer and she found it hard to pronounce some words. And soon her swallowing and breathing would have been affected. So all of those things combined were much more important than the pain she was in. She was an incredibly stoic person.

Elizabeth was very direct in her speech and she didn't hide her feelings. She had certainly said, "You know, when this gets to a certain point I'm not going to be here. You've got to know that. One of these days—I can't tell you when, because then you might be considered implicated—I just won't be here."

Once her mind was made up, she had made it up forever,

unless there were really good, prevailing reasons why she should change it. But she was a cheerful, outgoing, incredibly alive person. Right up until the end. So it was hard to know when her time would come. And she wasn't going to do it because she was depressed. She was going to do it because she'd have had enough and she didn't want to go any further in the direction in which she was going. But she hung on until she knew that paralysis was imminent and that was a place she just simply wasn't willing to go.

When I was a priest of the Anglican Church, nobody ever came to me and said "This is what I've chosen as my option," although there had been cases of people dying in great distress, where the doctor basically said "There's nothing I can do." That was of some concern to me. And so, years before Elizabeth had ever contracted MS, I had spoken in church, in the course of homilies and so on, about the possibilities of assisted dying.

My position is that it should be legalized and the Church should stop being so silly about its attitude toward suffering people. I've always taken that point of view. I have never had anybody say to me, "No, I don't think that should be permitted." Not one. And I spoke about it often enough that people in the Church knew where I stood. Actually, it was just after the first time I said this that the General Synod of the Anglican Church of Canada adopted a report that said assisted dying—they probably called it "euthanasia," but I don't know that—was a failure of community and that it shouldn't be legalized. I wrote a response to the report and gave it to the primate and the author of the report, but I never heard back from them.

There was a possibility, with the Anglican Church, for holding fairly diverse points of view on most issues of importance. So it wasn't a question of anybody disciplining me for raising issues of that kind. It was not likely to happen, but they certainly didn't endorse what I'd said, and they didn't respond to my concerns about the report that had been adopted.

You wouldn't have called me an orthodox Christian. You might call me a radical theologian in some respects, and I became more radical as the years went by. In fact, shortly before my retirement was due, I had a priest friend who was retired in the parish and he used to say to me, "Slow down, you're going to talk yourself out of a job."

But from the first time that I went to that parish [in Middleton, a town in Nova Scotia's Annapolis Valley]— Elizabeth and I were both there for fourteen years—I said, "I am a modern theologian, I read a lot of theology and I have a lot of questions. So I'll raise a lot of questions."

Elizabeth had a lot of other issues with the Church over the years. I might add that her memorial service was not held in a church and it was not a religious service, at her request. In fact I still have some of her written instructions about exactly what was to happen and what I was to do. Normally, in the case of the death of a spouse of a priest, the bishop would take the service; that's his prerogative, and normally that's what would have happened. But she wrote letters to the bishop basically saying that this wasn't going to happen. The role of the Church in her life had changed over the years and she would rather have a non-religious service.

Our own faith journey, if you want to call it that, sort of went step by step, because as the years went by I found it more and more difficult to say positive things about the readings that were prescribed for the day—for Sundays and holy days. And people knew I was struggling with that. In fact, a layperson in the parish said, "One of the most interesting things was to watch you lose your faith in public over the last two or three years."

The only thing that relieved Elizabeth's symptoms and some of the spasticity was a drug called Dantrium. She took it in fairly large quantities. Eventually, in April of 2006, she had severe liver failure. She was jaundiced, a very yellowish colour—I think it was a kind of golden oak colour. She went into the hospital and she got a little bloated and there was some question of whether she was going to live. When she got out of the hospital in May, she never recovered her ability to move and transfer on her own from the bed to the wheelchair and so on, and she just lost all function below her arms. At that point, she began to think very seriously about where this was going.

Anniversaries were always important to Elizabeth, and on September 6, 2006, which was the anniversary of her first symptom, she tried to do it. She was a card-carrying pot smoker—one of the people who were given permission—but I'm allergic to the smoke. So she had her own room, not a bedroom, but a kind of an office with her desk and her computer and that sort of thing. And every evening at seven she used to go into her room and smoke pot. And then she would come out. She had this all planned and worked up, you see, so we would have our supper and watch TV and then she went into her room. She had a lot of morphine capsules that came in huge bottles, and when she stopped taking them she still had a lot left. Unfortunately—or fortunately, as things may be—she didn't grind them up and they were time-released.

When I went in, she was slumped over her desk. She had taped a message on her back, basically saying, "There's a stethoscope" (we had given our daughter a stethoscope for Christmas one time, because she had professed herself interested in becoming a veterinarian, so we thought that would be a nice gift) "so check and see. If I'm dead, call the funeral home director."

I was in pretty desperate straits at the time and I kind of panicked. But I phoned the doctor and she said, "Well, she told you there was a stethoscope. Why don't you take it and see if her heart is still beating." So I did, and it was. And the doctor said, "She's left strict instructions that she's not to be resuscitated, so we'll just have to wait." That was something the doctor was quite prepared to respect.

I moved Elizabeth onto the bed, because she had been slumped over on the desk. And I just slept with her for the next thirty-six hours until she woke up.

She was very disoriented and confused. For a few hours, her speech was slurred and she would say absolutely nonsensical things. That was late evening, but the next morning when she woke up, she was back almost to normal again, although very disappointed that what she had tried hadn't worked.

It was immediately after that she said to me, "Obviously this is not going to work. I'm not going to do that again." She said it was hard enough to do it once, to die alone, and she didn't want to try it twice.

Dying alone, that was not a nice thing to have to do, so she said, "If you can be there, we'll go to Switzerland." We'd talked about it beforehand, but she'd just said we couldn't afford it. Besides that, she had already said quite clearly that she was a Canadian through and through, and leaving Canada was a hard thing for her to do. She felt devastated to have to leave her country in order to do this.

If she'd been able to do it here in Canada, she would have lived longer. I told her, "I've said to you before that if that's what you want to do, I'll go with you." But one of the reasons that I didn't want to do that, really, was that it meant that she was going to have to abbreviate her life, because she had to be able to travel in order to do this, and at some point that wasn't going to be possible except in an air ambulance, and that would have been way out of our reach.

I don't know a lot about the preparations; she did them all. That's what I told her when she said, "I would like for you to be there." I said, "Fine, I'll do that. I'll go with you, but I can't make the arrangements. It would be like me killing you myself. I just … I can't do that."

She was still able to speak, but it was getting harder. Her voice had become quite gravelly, and she found it more and more difficult to pronounce certain words—longer words tended to be difficult, words with several syllables. But she made all the arrangements by email and by phone.

Around the end of October, she had all the documentation, all the application forms and so on, and had written a letter to Dignitas requesting what they called an "accompanied death." Then it was a matter of waiting for what they called a "provisional green light." They would take her documents, consider them themselves, and give all the medical documentation to a local physician, who would then get back to them about his willingness to see her. The doctor would not promise to prescribe the barbiturates until he had seen her, but they would send her back a provisional green light.

It was an anxious, anxious time for Elizabeth when she was waiting to hear back from Dignitas about whether they would accept her, because she was quite aware during this whole period that her MS hadn't stopped getting progressively worse. So she was quite concerned and very anxious.

In probably early January 2007, they gave her a provisional green light and a number of possible dates when she could see the doctor and a subsequent date on which she would have an accompanied death, if the doctor agreed. That was the first night that Elizabeth slept through the night, except when I had to turn her over. It was the first time in a long while that she was really able to sleep.

She didn't want to travel during the winter and she thought she could hang on until the spring. June 7 and 8 was the latest she felt confident she would be able to go, because of the way her disease was progressing. She was not confident, in fact, that she could last much longer.

A week or two before she was due to go, she was doing fairly well—she seemed to be doing fairly well from my point of view. So I said, "Look, you could stay. They're not going to refuse you. You could stay until September or October; there's no reason you need to go now." She just looked at me and said, "I'm sorry. I've got to go."

She spoke to Dignitas about the types of things that were required and what she would need. She booked flights, she booked hotels. She made all the arrangements for her memorial service. She chose the day that her memorial service would be held. She wanted to know where her ashes were going to be buried, so we bought plots in the cemetery close by here in Windsor, and we designed the stone and had it made and erected, so she saw to all that before she left. It was very impor-tant for her.

She spoke to a funeral home in Zurich. I couldn't believe it. I was sitting here one day at my desk and she was lying in the bed in the bedroom down the hall and she was on the phone. She used the phone regularly to speak with her friends, acquaintances, and this day she was talking to somebody in Zurich. I didn't know who it was, and then suddenly—I wasn't listening closely, I wasn't eavesdropping on her conversation—she said in this rather cheerful voice, "Well, that's good, that's good. You'll be seeing me, but I won't be seeing you!"

When the pilot said, "We have now left Canadian airspace," she breathed a sigh of relief. She had a sense that somebody might try to stop her before she got away from Canada. For her, it was kind of an escape. She didn't know whether anybody could stop her from doing this.

I guess the truth is we both had to be strong for each other. And we were, in a sense, cool. The dread really only came over me, I suppose, when we landed in Zurich. That's when the sense of … just the heavy, heavy dread. Except for the night before—the evening of the seventh, when we let all our guards down and let it all pour out—except for that, we were fairly disciplined about the whole thing. Very disciplined, in fact.

The doctor was actually not in Zurich. He was in a suburb of Zurich, in a village called Schwerzenbach. So we went out to see the doctor, and he spoke to her for, I suppose, an hour, hour and a half. It was very obvious that the MS was very far advanced. So he apparently had no problem. What he did then, of course, was he prescribed the drug, or, as they call it in German, the *medicament*. And the people from Dignitas would administer it.

We had our hotel in Zurich and we had arranged for a limo service so we wouldn't have to navigate our own way around the city and find things. He met us at the airport and took us to our hotel. He picked us up later that afternoon and took us to Schwerzenbach, to the doctor, and then he took us for a sightseeing drive, basically around the lake and different places in Zurich.

We went out that evening and had supper, then came back to the hotel and let everything hang out for a while, because we needed some chance to really face up to what we were doing.

In the morning, we had breakfast and I took her in her wheelchair and we walked around that part of Zurich where we were, chatted all the while, and there was never … I mean, there were tears before, we had a good cry the night before, but that day not a tear. And not a word that would indicate that what was coming was something to be dreaded.

Then our driver picked us up and took us to Gertrudstrasse, where the Dignitas apartment was. When we got to the apartment, there were a number of legal documents that had to be signed, basically to say we knew what we were doing there and we agreed that Dignitas should do what they were doing.

They wanted to talk with Elizabeth. And during that conversation—and it was just a general conversation about things—but during the conversation, Herr Bernhard [a social worker who is a Dignitas "escort"] several times said to Elizabeth, "You know, you don't have to do this. You can go back to Canada if you want and nobody will think less of you if you decide not to do this." The point was to make sure there was no hesitation in Elizabeth's mind and she wasn't indecisive about it. After he had said this several times and Elizabeth had assured him, "No, this is why I came to Switzerland," and it didn't really seem as though they were going to stop, Elizabeth said, "Well, isn't it just about time we got going?"

He said, "If that's what you wish." And Elizabeth said, "That's what I'm here for." And so then he explained the process, which is basically this: The barbiturates are very bitter and they also have a tendency to make a person feel nauseous, so the first stage is to provide an anti-nausea medication. He mixed that and gave it to Elizabeth to drink, and she did. And then you have to wait half an hour for it to take effect. And during that half-hour we chatted away as we had before. And toward the end—we must have been forty minutes or so— Elizabeth said, "Isn't it about time we were getting on to the next stage?" And so she was directive all the way through, and I don't know whether that was intentional on their part or not, or whether it was just that Elizabeth tended to be very sort of directive and decisive about these things herself. But she said, you know, "It's time to get on with this."

And so he said, "Okay. What I'm going to do is to mix the medication. It has to settle for about five minutes and you have to mix it up." There was a sink and a water bottle and so on in the room, and so he went over and he mixed the medication. Then he said, "Now we'll let that settle for five minutes." Then she wanted to do two things. She said, "Is there a garbage can in the room?" And he said, "Yes, right over there." She had a number of things she wanted to get rid of, things that symbolized for her, her—I don't know—her whole journey with her disease. Included were some orthopedic shoes, a brace for her leg—a couple of braces for her legs—all her drugs, and so on. As she threw them away, she said—you'll have to excuse my language; Elizabeth was fairly rough and ready when it came to her language, especially in later years—as she put them into the wastepaper basket, she threw them in, and she said, "Fuck this." And then she threw the next thing in, and she said, "Fuck that," until she was through with disposing of all these things that symbolized what had happened to her. "Now," she said, "I'm ready."

And she said, "Can I get on the bed?" There was a bed in the room, and so she lay on the bed. And Arthur Bernhard said, "I have to video the next part of what we're going to do." He said, "I'll set this video machine up on the tripod, and then I will say to you, 'If you drink this, you will die.' And while my assistant hands it to you, you must answer me to the effect that you know this."

He set it up and he tried to make it go, but it didn't work. He said, "Excuse me, I have another one upstairs." So he left the room. Elizabeth and I said our goodbyes at that point, still very controlled—I mean, that was one thing she had said: "I want this to be a dignified thing. I don't want this to be a time of tears or anything like that." So it was very controlled.

Gabriella [a Dignitas volunteer] was still in the room and that was okay. We were quite oblivious to the presence of other people at that point. So we just hugged and kissed and said our goodbyes. And then she got back on the bed and he came back with the camera. There was a chair at the head of the bed, but it was out of view of the camera, so I went and sat in the chair. He set the camera up, he took the little plastic glass with the drugs in it and gave it to Gabriella and she handed it to Elizabeth. And then Gabriella stood out of the way, and while Elizabeth was holding the glass and looking into the camera, Arthur said to her, "Mrs. MacDonald, if you drink this you will die." And she said, "I understand that." And she drank it down, just like that. I mean, there wasn't any hesitation between "I understand that" and drinking it. She drank it right down. It was very bitter, and Gabriella gave her a glass of water, so she drank some and she lay back on the bed and I lay on the bed with her and cradled her head in my arm.

We were listening to music that she had chosen. It was Snow Patrol's "Chasing Cars." She rather liked the song, so that's what she had playing. And I just … I said goodbye. I said, "I love you," and she said, "I love you too." And she grasped my hand.

After about five minutes, I suppose, she went to sleep. And about ten minutes later, she was gone. Very rapid and very quiet. We lay there together until Arthur came over. He just said quietly to me, "I think she's gone." And then I looked down and said, "Yeah, I think she has too."

I knew that it was something she was determined to do, and I think she had good reason to do it. I don't know whether you'd call it a comfort being there, but it was a reassurance that she didn't suffer as she died and she's not suffering now.

11 The Death We Want
Debating the future of the negotiated death

IN LATE JUNE 2003, Joyce Holland, an octogenarian with advanced Alzheimer's disease, began to swallow her food into her lungs instead of her stomach. Noticing that she was in distress, the staff at the long-term care facility where she lived sent her to Toronto Western Hospital. Along with aspiration pneumonia, she suffered from recurring infections and her lungs required suctioning to remove the buildup of phlegm. She'd also developed severe and painful bedsores as well as contractures, or locked joints.

After a little more than a week, as her condition worsened, doctors transferred Holland to the intensive care unit and placed her on a ventilator to help her breathe, then gave her antibiotics to treat the infections and inotropic drugs to raise her blood pressure. She made it out of the ICU a month later, but returned after only a week because she was suffering from pneumonia and an infection caused by an intravenous tube. Again she needed the ventilator and the inotropic drugs, but after another month she returned to a ward.

Holland, a former postal worker, couldn't speak, but she could hear and would open her eyes and look at the speaker when someone said her name. Her daughters, Patricia and Margaret, believed she recognized them and was aware of their presence and they thought she was able to watch television. None of the doctors and nurses who treated her had seen any evidence of that, but they agreed that she was conscious and not in a coma or a vegetative state.

After Holland moved out of intensive care the first time, some members of the medical team discussed whether it made sense to send her back if she faltered again; after the second time, the team became convinced that the burdens she'd bear by returning to the ICU outweighed the benefits. The ventilator helped her breathe, but it was uncomfortable and took a "terrible toll" on her, according to Holland's critical care doctor, Laura Hawryluck, and the intravenous tubing needed to administer the inotropic drugs added to her discomfort.

Hawryluck wasn't just a doctor; she'd completed a master's in bioethics and had taught, written on and spoken about end-of-life care and decision making. She met with Holland's two daughters in September and suggested that rather than sending their mother on another trip to the ICU, the best course of action would be to keep her as comfortable as possible with painkillers and sedatives. Under the doctor's proposal, Holland's feeding tube would stay attached and the hospital would continue suctioning mucus from her lungs, but she wouldn't get life-sustaining treatments such as going back on the ventilator or the inotropic drugs or, if her heart failed, receiving cardiopulmonary resuscitation. Hawryluck asked the daughters for their consent.

The meeting clearly upset the women, and though they felt intimidated, they refused to give their consent. They wanted to respect their mother's wishes, and what the doctor was asking for wouldn't do that since it likely meant that the next time their mother took a turn for the worse would be the last.

Holland had given her daughters powers of attorney for personal care in 1998. Two years earlier, her husband had died of

Alzheimer's disease and she had been disturbed and disappointed by the level of medical support he had received. So while she hadn't filled out a living will or had a detailed and specific discussion with her daughters about what should or should not be done, she had made it clear she wanted her life prolonged. Holland's faith was important to her. A Roman Catholic, she believed in the sanctity of life and often used the expression "Where there's life there's hope."

After the daughters refused the medical team's proposal, Hawryluck made an application to the Consent and Capacity Board (CCB), an independent tribunal in Ontario that holds hearings on disputes over capacity, consent and substitute decision making. The CCB mostly reviews involuntary status in psychiatric facilities under the *Mental Health Act*, but it also considers people's capacity to consent to treatment or refuse it under the *Health Care Consent Act*. Hawryluck wanted the board to decide if, by demanding further life-sustaining treatment, the daughters were really representing their mother's best interests.

By the time the CCB panel heard the case in October, Holland's lungs had to be suctioned every forty-five minutes or so and she had continued to develop infections and fevers that required antibiotics, but she had not gone back to intensive care and was, according to Hawryluck, "holding her own." The doctor told the board she didn't know if Holland would last longer than six months to a year, but under cross-examination she agreed that the woman's condition was stable and said that Holland was deteriorating more slowly than she would have expected. Still, she believed her patient had experienced discomfort, pain and loss of dignity in intensive care and pointed out that the treatment had no effect on the Alzheimer's, which would ultimately kill her even if she survived her next bout in the ICU.

Although the board found that the daughters could not be faulted for advancing what they understood to be "her wishes, values, beliefs and interests," it decided that Holland's request to be kept alive had been too general to apply to the situation she would later find herself in. The board sided with the medical team and ordered the women to consent to no further life-supporting treatment for their mother.

But the daughters appealed to the Ontario Superior Court, and later in October, while the board's ruling was under appeal, Holland went back into the ICU and onto a ventilator. Her level of ventilator support decreased between November and December but increased again in January. Still, since she was able to breathe spontaneously, she was on moderate, rather than full, ventilator support. And while she'd recovered from the pneumonia, her neurological condition remained the same.

When the Superior Court heard the case, in January 2004, the attorney general of Ontario and the Euthanasia Prevention Coalition (EPC) were interveners. The trial was originally scheduled to take two days, but Justice Maurice Cullity agreed to extend it so the court could hear all the arguments.

The Euthanasia Prevention Coalition, which opposes the legalization of euthanasia or assisted suicide and promotes palliative care, viewed the situation as a David versus Goliath battle; the Holland family was up against the high-powered lawyers representing Hawryluck and the attorney general. According to executive director Alex Schadenberg, the organization intervened in the case because it believed that health care teams shouldn't be allowed to withhold or withdraw medical treatment from patients against their previously expressed wishes and that there should be "a presumption in favour of life." In addition, since Holland was not brain dead or on life support, the EPC worried that the Consent and Capacity Board ruling, if not overturned, would be "a significant step down the slippery slope towards professionally assisted euthanasia or mercy killing."

Although Cullity overturned the board's ruling, the ordeal was emotionally draining for Holland's daughters. Not only did they have to publicly expose their private sadness and struggle, but they faced some tough questioning from the CCB. The chair of the panel asked one daughter if she could imagine situations where her mother might change her views on the need to prolong life. When she said she couldn't think of any, the chair asked, "Suppose prolonging her life cost the life of one of her children; is that something she would want?" The process was also financially draining—lawyers are expensive and Cullity did not award any damages in the case.

For the EPC, the case was a victory, but not the precedent-setting one it had hoped for. Because Cullity found that the board had made errors in law and in fact, he decided not to consider the arguments under Canada's *Charter of Rights and Freedoms*, stating that those issues should be determined in subsequent cases. "The EPC is happy that Holland is now protected from death," noted Schadenberg, "and also recognizes that the greater battle has just begun."

For Hawryluck, the case not only added to the confusion over end-of-life issues, it left her wondering how to balance her duty to families demanding painful treatments with her duty not to inflict unnecessary pain. "It tears you apart on so many levels it's hard to explain," she told the *Ottawa Citizen*. "You don't want to cause the family grief, yet you don't want to cause your patient grief. So what do you do?"

LIKE SO MANY other end-of-life disputes that wind up in court, the Holland case failed to provide any useful standard for the future. When health care professionals look to the legal system for clarity on these dilemmas, judges usually decide, quite reasonably, that they're not experts in medicine, ethics or the end of life and suggest that the people who are should be the ones to sort out these matters. But the easiest way to provoke an argument in a room full of doctors is to ask, "When you have an end-of-life case involving an incapable patient in the ICU, who should make the final decision—the family or medical team?" Even from hospital to hospital, there are disparities: at some, the guidelines give doctors the right to withhold treatment; at others, doctors will maintain the treatment while continuing their attempts to convince the family to see the situation the way they do.

That inconsistent approach certainly doesn't prevent conflict. In 2008, Anand Kumar decided to quit working as a doctor in the critical care unit at Winnipeg's Grace Hospital rather than continue treating eighty-four-year-old Samuel Golubchuk. Five years earlier, Golubchuk had suffered severe brain damage in a fall. By late 2007, he was alive only with the help of a ventilator and a feeding tube. Whether or not he was barely above a vegetative state, as the hospital contended, became a matter of some dispute when the case made it to court, but his brain function was certainly limited.

After Kumar recommended taking the man off life support, Golubchuk's son and daughter—who, like their father, were Orthodox Jews and believed pulling the plug would be a sin—obtained a temporary order to continue treatment until the case could be heard at a trial. Months later, the patient's bedsores were so bad that doctors had to cut diseased flesh from his body to prevent the infection from spreading. "This is grotesque," Kumar wrote in his resignation letter to the Winnipeg Regional Health Authority. "To inflict this kind of assault on him without a reasonable hope of benefit is an abomination. I can't do it."

Soon, two of his colleagues also refused shifts at the hospital rather than be forced to treat Golubchuk. Earlier that year, the Manitoba College of Physicians and Surgeons had released "Withholding and Withdrawing Life-Sustaining Treatment," a policy that called for doctors to consult with family members, but in a break from other provinces, gave the ultimate decision about taking someone off life support to the medical professionals. Nevertheless, the judge who granted the temporary order concluded: "Contrary to the assertion of the defendants [Grace Hospital], it is not settled law that, in the event of disagreement between a physician and his patient as to withdrawal of life supports, the physician has the final say." Any chance to end the confusion slipped away when Golubchuk died in late June, before the September trial date.

So once again, clear as blood. Kerry Bowman, who actually consulted on the Hawryluck conflict during the early stages, doesn't think going to court with either the Holland or Golubchuk dispute made much sense. The ideal case for a hospital to pursue would involve a capable patient who, before he can no longer communicate, clearly tells a doctor, nurse or clinical ethicist in a documented conversation that he doesn't want a certain treatment. When the adult children, who may be more religious than their father, want the medical team to do everything to keep him alive and are willing to fight in court, then the hospital likely has a winnable case, because legally and ethically it doesn't matter what the kids want, only what the father said he wanted. And the Canadian medical system needs to win some of these cases to set precedents.

But if we're looking to judges or doctors for the answer, we're looking to the wrong people. For now, hospitals still manage to avoid disputes most of the time and settle the majority of the conflicts that do arise. With an aging population, though, not to mention the threat of pandemics, ignoring the need for greater clarity in these situations is reckless. In the absence of more useful legislation on negotiating death, reluctant judges will eventually decide something. And while I've never been the type to whine about judicial activism—which is invariably just an epithet ideologues use when they don't like a court's decision— we do need to settle this ourselves with a public debate.

WHEN SIMON SMITH asked me to moderate a bioethics debate, I said yes. A former student of mine, Smith went on to launch Betterhumans.com, a website devoted to transhumanism. I had only a foggy notion of what that was, but I suspected it wasn't quite as simple as "a bunch of people who want to have micro-chips implanted in their heads," which is how one of Smith's old classmates had mischievously explained it to me.

Actually, transhumanism is a philosophy that promotes technology as the best way to improve the human condition. And the event, entitled "Debating the Future: Bioethics from Science Fiction to Science Fact," featured four questions: Should we ban cloning? Do we need a moratorium on the development of nanotechnology? Will life extension offer more benefit than harm? Should parents have the right to modify their children's genes? I was intrigued by the questions and impressed by the two debaters Smith had recruited.

One was Margaret Somerville, someone that the late, great radio host Peter Gzowski—who met or interviewed a lot of people in his lifetime— called "the smartest woman in Canada." She is a professor of both law and medicine at McGill University and is the founding director of the McGill Centre for Medicine, Ethics and Law. She also writes books, op-ed pieces and letters to the editor—and she's certainly not afraid to take unpopular and controversial stands on everything from male circumcision (against) to same-sex marriage (against) to euthanasia (against). Those positions have earned her a reputation as a hardcore conservative, though she bristles at the suggestion: "I'm not, but neither am I a liberal. Because of the nature of my work as an ethicist—while realizing that one's own personal values are always an influence—I have never taken a 'package approach' to the values that should govern the ethical issues that I debate in the public square." In her book *The Ethical Canary: Science, Society and the Human Spirit*, she argues that whatever breaches two values—respect for life, especially human life, and respect for the human spirit—is inherently wrong. "Scientific progress alone would be a hollow victory," she writes, "without the moral and ethical progress that must accompany it and ensure the humanization and humanity of our development and use of science."

If Somerville is cautious about technology and the future, James Hughes, her opponent that night, is impatient. In fact, the self-styled "Dr. J" believes "the future can be very fun, and that everybody can have lots of new toys." A professor at Trinity College in Hartford, Connecticut, Hughes is a one-time Buddhist monk, founding editor of a zine called the *EcoSocialist Review* and author of papers with titles such as "Embracing Change With All Four Arms: A Post-Humanist Defence of Human Genetic Engineering." A cofounder of the World Transhumanist Association, he's the poster boy for what Somerville calls the "techno-utopians." He's claimed to be a profound feminist with a serious distaste for his own sex. And he's happily taken many controversial positions, including having years ago dismissed as "so last week" the debate over same-sex marriage (true in Canada, perhaps, but certainly not south of the border) and arguing for a system that would allow up to five people to enter into cohabitation or child-rearing contracts.

With two intelligent, knowledgeable and outspoken people grappling with four fascinating questions, I figured it all sounded like good fun and I was looking forward to playing my modest role as moderator. At least I was until the morning of the debate, when *The Globe and Mail* published op-ed pieces from Somerville and Hughes. As I read them, I began to fear that these two people weren't even speaking the same language. Surely, I thought, they need an interpreter, not a moderator.

Coincidentally, the debate took place in the same room at the University of Toronto where I'd seen Leon Kass speak several months earlier. In 2001, Kass became one of the most powerful ethicists in the world when George W. Bush picked the medical doctor and University of Chicago professor to head the President's Council on Bioethics. Not surprisingly, given who had named him to the post (which he held for four years), Kass was a bioconservative with strong positions against embryonic stem-cell research, in-vitro fertilization and many other issues. In his lecture, entitled "Why Not Immortality?", he praised the virtues of mortality. And while he claimed his position was not based on religion, it sure sounded like it to me—not least because his suggestion that life is incomplete without children is a profoundly conservative and faith-based notion. In addition, he seemed to be using the case against immortality (and, really, who wants to live *forever*?) to make the case against life extension. At one point, he asked if a tennis player would want to play 25 percent more games of tennis, suggesting the answer was a rather obvious no. I immediately thought of Bjorn Borg, the Swedish great who dominated the sport in the seventies. He retired in 1981 and then made three ill-fated attempts at a comeback, in the early nineties, which seemed evidence enough that yes, indeed, he did want to play more. And anyway, there's an awfully big difference between wanting to play more and wanting to live forever. That's why I was so delighted that during the question-and-answer session after the lecture, author and U of T history professor Michael Bliss pointed this out, suggesting we had witnessed some "verbal sleight of hand." His question, more than anything Kass had to say, was the highlight of the event.

I was completely unpersuaded by Kass's ideological argument. In addition, many procedures we take for granted (the removal of an appendix, for example) are forms of life extension and no reasonable person is going to argue against them. But I also knew that some ethicists had legitimate concerns about this issue, such as whether our ability to stay healthy would keep pace with our potential to live longer, whether longer lives would only go to those who could afford them and, that old chestnut, whether we should be playing God. James Hughes, on the other hand, was arguing for radical life extension or even immortality—though several times I wondered if he really meant all the things he said in the debate, because some of them were pretty out there. Still, I didn't expect much in the way of fireworks, as I didn't imagine that Somerville and Hughes would be that far apart on this issue.

But clash they did. Somerville, whose red reading glasses and mod-looking haircut with blond streaks made her seem younger and groovier than she appears on the news, began her comments by saying, "Well, this is the toughest issue to debate and quite frankly the transhumanists make the sirens of old look like amateurs when they start talking about life extension and immortality." But this discussion was also the most fascinating point in the evening, because in a way the four questions became irrelevant and the two debaters got down to talking about how they really differed. "Where our clash of worldviews comes in, between James and me," said Somerville, "is do you really believe there's something inherently good in the natural? And I do."

A couple of months later, I visited Somerville, whom most people call Margo, in her office at the Centre for Medicine, Ethics and Law in a beautiful old building on Montreal's Peel St., part way up Mount Royal. When I arrived, she was sitting at her computer in a huge office lined with books. She was eating soup and had forgotten I was coming, but she quickly welcomed me in and she sat on a blue-and-purple couch in front of the windows in the turret of the building.

At first, we talked about the debate: "I'm really committed to what I call a basic presumption in favour of respect for the natural," she said. "James's is a basic presumption in favour of technology." Somerville believes there are four possible starting points when making ethical decisions: (1) No, it's prohibited entirely; (2) Yes, do what you like; (3) No, don't do it unless you can be sure that it's ethical and it's not going to cause physical or moral harm either to a person or to a broader society or to future generations; and (4) Yes, but if you find out it's really harmful, then stop doing it. Somerville adheres to the third one, while Hughes, she believes, is committed to the fourth. She went on to suggest that the fascination transhumanists have with immortality and life extension is really a reaction to their fear of death.

Somerville, who grew up in Australia and went to Catholic girls' schools, got a pharmacy degree and worked as a pharmacist before setting up an antiques business. After becoming "mad keen about cooking," she wrote a chapter of a cookbook. When she and her then husband moved to New Zealand, she taught agricultural science at a high school for boys ("one of the most terrifying jobs I've had in my whole life") before returning to

Sydney and studying law. She practised litigation until her husband got a post-doc in medical research at McGill in 1975. She reluctantly gave up the job she loved and followed him to Montreal, where she did a Ph.D. in medicine, ethics and law. It was, in a weird way, a natural combination, given her Catholic schooling and her experience in pharmacy and the legal world. But in the mid-seventies it was unusual indeed.

Today, Somerville—who mused that if she were starting out now, she might go into journalism—is the best-known ethicist in Canada. To people in the media, she is an indispensable source, in part because she is one of the few ethicists who understands what reporters do (and it doesn't hurt that she actually likes many of them). She does over 250 interviews a year, including as many as 30 in a week when a big ethical issue breaks. That media profile rubs some people the wrong way; several years ago the CBC received a letter from a viewer who threatened to throw a brick through his TV if he saw her on it again. It's also led to resentment and jealousy on the part of some other ethicists; one griped to me, "A lot of journalists have just one number in their Rolodex, and it's hers."

Despite all the interviews she's done over the years, Somerville says she's never been misquoted, quoted out of context or had a confidence breached. Not many people who've dealt with the media can claim such an unblemished record, but part of her good fortune is that she knows how to talk to reporters. After all, someone who talks in clear, simple and direct language is less likely to be misunderstood—and misquoted or misrepresented— than someone who speaks in convoluted sentences filled with academic jargon and lofty philosophical concepts.

I asked her why she did so much media work, and right away she said, "Oh, clearly there's an ego thing involved." But she also believes in the value of public debate and thinks ethicists have an important role in it. "There's no point in being an ethicist in the closet."

Her red-framed glasses sat on top of her head and she wore a tight black T-shirt. She moved around a lot as we talked, sometimes leaning back so far she was almost reclining, other times sitting up straight or leaning forward. Somerville is a warm, friendly person; when I was leaving, I thought she was going to hug me. She has an easy laugh and an obvious enthusiasm for life—and conversation.

When I asked her how much power and influence she thought ethicists have, she said that when the people with the real power agree with them, "then it seems as though you have lots of power. When they don't, there are various ways in which you're handled." That's when people use the derogatory labels: difficult, controversial, neo-Luddite, too religious, too secular, too right-wing, too left-wing. A staunch defender of gay rights, she came out against same-sex marriage, and people would say to her, "What's happened to you? We thought you were in our camp." But she intentionally doesn't belong to a camp, refuses to join organizations and refuses to let her name be attached to campaigns or petitions.

She did say yes to a human rights award for her stand against male circumcision, but her acceptance speech at Oxford University supported a religious exemption and spurred a third of the audience to stand up and boo. As she told me about this, she got up from the couch, walked across the room, her shoes clicking on the hardwood floor, and grabbed a copy of *The Ethical Canary*. She began reading a section that listed all the people who were furious: the anti-circumcision movement; Jews and Muslims; feminists; physicians; parents; and "one young man who was an anti-circumcision activist from Tel Aviv who accused me of being anti-Semitic because my proposal for an exemption for religious belief meant that I was willing to protect all newborn baby boys in the world except Jewish ones."

I assumed she enjoyed getting a rise out of people, especially given the conventional wisdom that anyone who receives flak from all sides is doing something right. But the charge that she seeks controversy particularly offends Somerville, because it diminishes her positions, and she didn't enjoy the circumcision storm at all. "I went through hell," she said, adding that big donors to the university even threatened to cut off all future donations if Bernard Shapiro—then McGill's principal and later the federal ethics commissioner—didn't fire her. (He didn't, of course, citing academic freedom.)

Outspoken ethicists may get heated responses the way activists do, but that's not the way Somerville sees her job. She's happy to spark debate, but she's not out to change the world—unless, of course, it's to make it a more ethical place. "I have an enormous privilege. I'm paid to sit and think and write and say what I believe. But I can't be an activist because that means I've joined a gang, and I can't do that because it's not my role. In fact, it's antithetical to my role."

PERHAPS THE ONE THING people on both sides of the ethical divide can agree on is that if Terri Schiavo had to die, starving her to death was not the most humane way to go. "Psychologically, it is a nightmare," said Kerry Bowman. "It also raises the great question of why can't we take another look at euthanasia, because why should anyone ever have to starve to death if the end result is the same?"

While as a clinical ethicist, Bowman could not stand by and watch someone perform euthanasia because it's illegal, as a public issue ethicist he's happy to be outspoken about wanting to see a debate about it. Sure, it's easy to dismiss a big debate as a delay tactic, especially since other countries, such as Belgium and the Netherlands, have already liberalized their laws. But reaching a consensus on such issues is easier in European nations that aren't as ethnically or culturally diverse as Canada. Besides, the debate has barely begun here. The majority of the families Bowman sees—regardless of their education level, mother tongue or country of origin—don't fully understand the legal and ethical aspects of end-of-life decisions. "They're not certain how the laws work and what is or isn't okay."

So far, the right to die hasn't exactly emerged as a roaring public issue, though there may be a rumble in the distance. Some health care workers admit they are too terrified of being prosecuted even to have a conversation with patients who raise the subject, and for a long time few ethics seminars or symposia would dare touch euthanasia or assisted suicide. But now braver folks are starting to open the discussion, albeit slowly and gingerly. When Bowman finds himself on a podium and brings it up, part of the audience, he can tell, is uncomfortable and wishes he would change the channel; others nod their heads. Good thing, too, especially with the aging of the baby boom generation, a rights-oriented bunch that won't accept any loss of power as their health declines. Boomers, who are less likely to defer to religious doctrine than previous generations, are already dealing with their parents—and are not at all impressed by what they're seeing. They are headed for the same fate, but they could suffer even more. Medical advances and healthier, more active lifestyles mean longer life expectancy but perhaps also longer declines. Someone whose father spent six debilitating years before dying at eighty-nine may be looking at a decade of incapacity before death at ninety-four.

Bowman's willingness to debate the death we want separates him from the doctors and ethicists who avoid the subject because they don't trust the general population's ability to make intelligent decisions about difficult matters. Meanwhile, most politicians are too frightened to touch it, presumably for fear there are more votes to lose than to gain. I don't just mean that in the casually cynical way that so many of us dismiss our politicians, because of course the people we elect care what we think. How else would they know what to say? Governments do poll, but polling is not consensus and it certainly isn't debate. Worse, a survey is just a snapshot of public opinion at a given time, and public opinion is fluid—especially on difficult issues.

The "yuck factor" describes our revulsion at a technological concept or advancement that seems to cross some ethical line. But what grosses us out today may seem perfectly acceptable in a few years. I was appalled in 1978 when I heard about the birth of Louise Brown, the world's first test-tube baby. Today, I think in-vitro fertilization (IVF) is perfectly normal and a great option for people who can't otherwise have a child. Because such shifts in attitude are common, Timothy Caulfield, a professor in both law and medicine at the University of Alberta and the research director of the Alberta Health Law Institute, believes laws are blunt instruments that should only be used when there is a high degree of consensus. "If history is any indication," he wrote in an op-ed piece in *The Globe and Mail*, "the public's attitude toward the prohibited activities will probably evolve. Research on cadavers was once considered an affront to human dignity; the announcement of the world's first 'test-tube' baby was met with a degree of repulsion, as was the prospect of heart transplants."

Time often helps reduce the yuck factor, but so does talking—and learning—about the subject. Part of my initial reaction to the birth of Louise Brown stemmed from my lack of knowledge about the IVF process. But our political leaders are wary of discussing controversial subjects unless they have no choice. Same-sex marriage became an issue only after several court rulings, and even then the federal government tried to wriggle out of a debate—and a decision—by referring the case to the Supreme Court of Canada. Without prodding from a court, the most a government is likely to do on issues such as euthanasia is study them, as it did in the mid-nineties with the Special Senate Committee on Euthanasia and Assisted Suicide. It's the handiest way to deal with a contentious issue, since it's not really dealing with it at all. Despite the pretense of seeking the public's opinion, such commissions certainly aren't a good way to generate public debate, because the people who show up tend to be the loudest and most strident advocates for each side.

That's where public issue ethicists could come in. Ideally, their role should be to educate and guide us through a debate on issues such as euthanasia and assisted suicide. "I personally believe that what I call 'doing ethics' is the obligation of everybody," Margaret Somerville said. "And if you go searching for ethics, you need some guides along the path. Everybody must be engaged in the ethical discourse. And one of the great needs at the moment is to try to work out how we can set up the public square or the public space that will allow as many voices to be heard as possible."

Caulfield, for one, believes that if they do their job properly, ethicists can be a trusted voice in debates when complex issues are not nearly as black and white as some insiders would like to present them. "From my incredibly conflicted position behind my academic desk here, I think we absolutely need ethicists," he told me. "You want that independent voice that can analyze these complex issues in a more dispassionate way."

When I asked him to grade the performance of Canadian ethicists, he wanted to pass on the question. But with a little prodding, he reluctantly admitted that they could be doing a better job. He regrets that some in his field get all uppity about who qualifies as a bioethicist. Caulfield, who has a law degree, doesn't think it's essential to have a Ph.D. in bioethics to contribute to the debate and would like to see more diversity of viewpoints, including those of anthropologists, sociologists and other philosophical disciplines as well as the legal community.

Second, ethicists must accept that the public won't always agree with them. Some opponents of therapeutic cloning, for example, were quick to dismiss opinion polls or focus groups that showed Canadians didn't have a problem with the research. "I find it frustrating that the exact same people who are calling for public engagement," he said, "often belittle any evidence that shows public support for something."

Third, ethicists shouldn't be afraid of the media. Some years, Caulfield gives up to a hundred interviews, and despite a couple of bad experiences he's generally been impressed with the journalists he's dealt with. What's more, he and his colleagues at the Health Law Institute have studied coverage of medicine and science and discovered reporters actually do a reasonably good job. Adults learn most of what they know about science, medicine and ethics from journalists, and even for those who follow up by doing their own research on the internet or elsewhere, the mainstream media probably first helped shape their views. "It's important for the whole academic community to be open to participating in that public debate," he said. "And you have to do that by getting involved in the popular press."

His constructive criticism aside, Caulfield admitted it's not easy to get a debate going. The media are obviously a crucial part of it, but ethicists and policy makers have to go further with citizens' juries and town halls as well as polling and focus groups. The problem is that none of these techniques are cheap and all have flaws. The people who show up at town hall meetings generally aren't the genuinely curious or responsible citizens who think they should learn about the matter before coming to a decision; they're the ones who've already made up their minds. "So how do you get a real public debate? That's a challenge that I don't have an answer for," he said. "Whether it's death and dying or other biotechnology issues—cloning or genetically modified organisms or xenotransplantation—I think that it is a real challenge for the social science community to figure out ways to meaningfully engage the public."

It doesn't help that the gulf between experts and the public has grown rather than shrunk. What began as a collective questioning of authority soon became contempt for authority. As one friend of mine said about ethicists, "Who died and made them God?"

Indeed, Eric Beresford, the former ethics consultant with the Anglican Church, told me he wasn't sure Canadians even needed people like him to lead the discussion. In 2001, he'd been part of a study on attitudes toward xenotransplantation, which is the process of putting animal cells, tissues or organs into humans. The study included both telephone polling and a series of town hall meetings across the country, with forty to fifty people representing a broad cross-section of the population at each meeting. It turned out that regardless of which experts were involved in the meetings, or how positive they had been about xenotransplantation, the exit polls showed no unqualified support for it. While Beresford admitted that ethicists can help make the discussion a bit more systematic, he was impressed by how the people who showed up at the meetings were able to tackle the ethical questions on their own. "What I saw was that people don't need an ethicist," he said. Not only does he worry that too often the debate is set up to exclude the general public, but he's also uncomfortable with the authoritarian edge to expertise. "I particularly worry about that in the area of ethics, precisely because we all think morally before anyone explains what moral thinking is. We're hard-wired for it."

Of course, Canadians rarely have a broad debate about any issue, let alone ethical ones. Certainly, we all thrashed out free trade in the late 1980s, and many people fretted over national unity for the first couple of decades of Quebec's independence movement. On the ethical front, though, any social event where people want to jaw about euthanasia and assisted suicide is probably not the kind of clambake any fun-loving person wants to attend.

But the way we deal with ethical dilemmas cuts to the values that shape us. Caulfield is fascinated with therapeutic cloning, which he admitted is a relatively marginal activity: few researchers work in the area, and any benefit that may come out of their work is probably decades away. "What's interesting about these debates is how they inform how we run our society, how we make decisions about the role of science and how we make decisions around morally contested issues in a pluralistic society. All those broader concerns are much more important than the more narrow substantive issue."

For their part, public issue ethicists need to be more willing to engage with us to get the debate going. Yes, that means taking risks, including trusting reporters and accepting it when the majority of people have a different view. For our part, citizens can't let their disdain for experts lead them to dismiss the contributions of ethicists. But at the same time, we need to trust ourselves—and reason for ourselves. After all, if we're hard-wired for making these decisions, as Eric Beresford suggests, all we have to do is educate ourselves, keep an open mind and let the debate begin.

GIVEN THAT MY FATHER died of cancer of the esophagus and his father died of stomach cancer, I've long feared that something gastrointestinal will eventually do me in. Shortly after I turned fifty, a doctor stuck an endoscope into my mouth and pushed it through my throat and down my gullet to my stomach for a little look-see. Turns out that not only did I have another ulcer (twenty years earlier a barium X-ray had revealed the first one I knew about), but I'd also developed Barrett's esophagus in the lower part of the tract between my throat and my stomach. Normally, the tissues in the linings of the esophagus and the intestines are quite different from each other, but intestine-type cells had replaced the normal ones.

The doctor explained his discovery to me, adding that my father probably had the same condition. But because of the "mild sedative" he'd given me, I was still quite stoned when we had our chat and later couldn't remember much. So, that afternoon, feeling a little more lucid, I looked up Barrett's esophagus on the internet and saw a disconcerting term: pre-cancerous. I knew that even decades after my father died of it, esophageal cancer was still nasty, so the way the doctor had put it—that I had only an increased chance of developing the disease—had come across as much less threatening. Either way, though, my youthful days of thinking I was immortal seemed long past.

As someone born in the back half of the great demographic bulge of the twentieth century, I'm often quick to point out all the ways I differ culturally from leading-edge baby boomers, but I'm not expecting much discrepancy in the way we approach death. Like our older cousins, members of my generation have done all we could to fight growing old, staying as active as our joints will let us, worrying about our diets and arguing over how much red wine is good for us and how much is too much. Though we all want to live a long, long time, the prospect of death doesn't scare us nearly as much as the prospect of dying badly. We want to go comfortably and painlessly and with as much of our dignity intact as possible.

I don't want religious leaders, or politicians playing to social conservatives, or even doctors deciding how I die. Just because I want the freedom to consider euthanasia or assisted suicide as an option doesn't mean everyone has to take advantage of that freedom. People who don't want doctors to pull the plug or drug them to death should talk to their family while still healthy, but so should those who don't want to spend fifteen years in a vegetative state surviving by feeding tube alone. And those who don't want a doctor to help them die without unnecessary suffering shouldn't ask for assisted suicide.

Opponents of liberalization go on and on about letting nature take its course and resisting the temptation to play God. But the surgeon who removed the diseased appendix from my five-year-old body wasn't letting nature take its course. (Good thing, too, or I wouldn't be around today.) We play God every day—pumping drugs, pulling plugs and a whole lot more—so what we're really fighting over is who gets to be the divine decider. Not that I am in any rush, but when my ride's here, I want to be the Supreme Being, because that's the best way to ensure I do go gently into that good night.

Acknowledgments

I DIDN'T START OUT to write a book about death. It's not a subject I knew much about or, truth be told, even one I ever really thought much about, especially since few people close to me have died. What I had planned to do was write about the role of ethicists in our society, but I kept following the most intriguing ethical dilemmas and wound up at the end of life. This journey took some time, and Diane Turbide, my initial editor, asked me several times if I wanted to bail out. So I'd like to thank her for standing by me when I wanted to keep going, as stubborn and foolhardy as I'm sure that seemed.

The challenge of editing the book fell to Alex Schultz, who helped me a lot with his keen eye, sensible advice and good humour. After Alex's scouring, copy editor Tara Tovell helped polish my writing (and my thinking). And Sandra Tooze shepherded it all through a tight production schedule. I'm also indebted to Chris Goldie, who read the first draft, as he always does, and Marg Falconer, who read the second. Any errors are, of course, mine alone.

My agent, David Johnston, did his usual great job of getting me more money than I deserve, Molly Duignan eased the pain with some research at crunch times, Heather Stonehouse saved me with some last-minute transcribing and several people, most notably Alex Wellington, helped me when I was trying to get my head around ethics and figure out what I was writing about.

Thanks also to Amy Spach; Moira Farr, Ian Pearson, Marni Jackson and the other friends of The Dave at the Banff Centre; Bill Reynolds and the rest of the gang at Ryerson; Simon Smith; Catherine Farquharson; Steve Watt; Gill Hawker; Paul MacDonald; and all my other ever-supportive friends and family members.

Special thanks to my mom. I hope the issues I explored in this book remain of nothing more than intellectual, rather than practical, interest to her for many years to come.

Most of all, thanks to Carmen Merrifield. Obviously.

Tim Falconer
Toronto
November 2008